THE ETERNAL HAPPINESS OF THE SAINTS

ST. ROBERT BELLARMINE

Translated by
REV. JOHN DALTON

CONTENTS

BOOK II

PREFATIO

ANNO superiore, ad meam præcipue spiritualem utilitatem, conscripsi mihi ipsum, libellum, De Ascensione Mentis in Deum, per Scalas Rerum Creatarum."[1] *Nunc, quoniam placet Deo senilem ætatem meam adhuc longius aliquantulum protrahere, subit animum de coelesti Patria, ad quam anhelamus omnes filii Adam, qui hanc vallem mortalitatis gementes et flentes incolimus, aliquid meditari, et meditationes stilo alligare, ne pereant. Igitur in Scripturis Sanctis, quæ sunt veluti Epistolæ Consolatorise de Patria Cœlesti ad exilium nostrum à Patre transmissse, quatuor nomina reperio, ex quibus utcunque bona illius Loci nobis innotescere possunt. Nomina sunt, Paradisus, Domus, Civitas, Regnum, &c.*

PREFACE

LAST year, for my own spiritual benefit especially, I composed a "Gradual to ascend unto God from the Contemplation of created objects." Now, since it hath pleased God to prolong my old age a little longer, I wish to meditate on that heavenly country to which all the sons of Adam ardently aspire, who dwell, lamenting and weeping, in this valley of death; and these meditations I desire to write, lest they perish. Wherefore in the Holy Scriptures, which may be compared to "Consoling Letters" sent unto us in this our exile from heaven by our Father, I find four names mentioned, from which we may in a manner learn what are the good things of that land. The names are, -Paradise, Mansion, City, and a Kingdom. Of Paradise St. Paul speaks: ***"I know a man in Christ above fourteen years ago such an one rapt even to the third heaven that he was caught up into paradise,"*** &c. Of the ***"Mansion"*** the Son of God himself speaks: ***" In my Fathers house there are many mansions."*** Of the ***"City"*** St. Paul speaks in his Epistle to the Hebrews: ***"But you are come to Mount Sion and the city of the living God,***

the heavenly Jerusalem." Of the *"Kingdom"* there is mention made in St. Matthew: *"Blessed are the poor in spirit, for theirs is the kingdom of heaven."*

This name is continually occurring in the Holy Scripture. The abode of the saints in heaven is called a "Paradise," because it is a most beautiful place, abounding in delights. But because men might suppose that paradise was a garden placed near a house, which could contain but few people, the Holy Spirit has added the name, "House," because it is a royal mansion, a great palace, wherein, besides a garden, there are halls, couches, and many other excellent things. But because a house, however large, cannot contain many people, and lest we should think that very few will possess eternal life, the Scripture adds the word "City," which contains many gardens and many palaces. But since St. John, speaking of the number of the blessed, saith: *"After this I saw a great multitude which no man could number."* And as, moreover, no city can contain an innumerable multitude, the word "Kingdom" is used, to which is added, "the kingdom of heaven" than which no place in the whole universe is more boundless and extensive.

But, again, since in a most extensive kingdom there are many who never see each other, nor know their names, nor whether they ever existed; and since it is certain that all the blessed behold each other, and know each other, and converse familiarly with one another as friends and relations: therefore the Scriptures, not content with the name of "Kingdom," added that of a "City," that we might know its inhabitants are truly citizens of the saints, and as familiar, and as closely united together, as the inhabitants of the very smallest city. But, in order that we might likewise remember, that these happy men are not only citizens of the saints, but also friends of God, therefore the Holy Spirit calls that a *"House,"* which it also named a *"City."*

In fine, because all the blessed in heaven abound in

delights, it is likewise called "Paradise." Hence these four words Kingdom, House, City, Paradise mean one and the same thing; and the Paradise is so extensive, that it can truly be called a House, City, and Kingdom. Wherefore, concerning this most blessed place I will first, under the word *"Kingdom";* then under that of a *"City* ;" afterwards under that of a *"House* ;" and, lastly, under the word *"Paradise"* meditate in the chamber of my heart; and, with God's assistance, commit to writing what He shall please to suggest unto me.

BELLARMINE

BOOK I

THE EXTENT OF THE KINGDOM OF GOD.

WE may learn how important is knowledge of the kingdom of heaven from this circumstance, that Christ our heavenly Master began His preaching with these words: "Do penance, for the kingdom of heaven is at hand." He also delivered nearly all His parables concerning the kingdom of heaven, saying, " The kingdom of heaven is likened & c. And after His resurrection, during the forty days before His ascension, appearing to His disciples, He spoke to them of the kingdom of God, as St. Luke mentions in the Acts of the Apostles. This kingdom therefore formed the beginning, continuation, and end of the discourses of Christ. But I do not intend to enter upon all the points connected with heaven, but only to explain those that relate to the "place and state" of the Blessed. In the first place, I will endeavour to show why the "habitation" of the blessed is called the "kingdom of heaven" in the Holy Scriptures.

The habitation of the saints is called a kingdom for many reasons. First, because it is a land the boundless extent of which cannot be conceived by human imagination. This earth, though but a point, as it were, in comparison with heaven, contains many and great kingdoms that can scarcely be numbered: how great, therefore, must that "one kingdom" be, which extends throughout the length and breadth of the heaven of heavens! But the kingdom of heaven does not only include the heavenly region, but also the whole extent of it. This heavenly country, which is properly called the kingdom of heaven, is the first "province," as it were, of the kingdom of God, in which the highest princes reside, who are all the sons of God. The second province may be called ætherial, in which the stars dwell; all of which, though not animate, yet are so obedient to the voice of their Creator, that they may be said to be living creatures, according to Ecclesiasticus, " Come, let us adore the King, for whom all things live”

The third province is aerial, in which winds and clouds pass, and storms, rain, snow, hail, thunder, and lightning are produced, and where birds of various kinds sport and fly. The fourth province is watery, and contains seas, fountains, and lakes, in which fishes multiply, “that pass through the paths of the sea." The fifth is earthly, which, emulous as it were of heaven, contains the most noble inhabitants, but not the most blessed I mean men, endowed with reason, but mortal; these have dominion over the beasts of the earth and the fishes of the sea. The last province is subterraneous, which, like the desert of Arabia, produces no good fruit whatever, but only thorns and briars; there wicked spirits dwell on account of their pride; they wished to be the first, but they became last they strove to exalt their throne above the stars of heaven, but they were cast down to the lowest hell. And here, also, those will be confined, who, having imitated the wickedness of those bad spirits, die without true repentance. Now, all these provinces God rules by His power, of whom the Psalmist speaks, " All things serve Thee” This vast and mighty kingdom God will share with those that love Him.

Wherefore, Christian soul, rejoice, and be not confined within the narrow limits of things present. Why dost thou labour and toil so much, merely to gain a small part of this world, whilst, if thou wish, thou canst possess the whole? Truly, if men would seriously aspire after this kingdom, if they would attentively meditate upon it, they would blush to wage war for such narrow portions of the earth. O man! God offers thee the possession of His immense and eternal kingdom, whilst thou fightest for one small city, wherein many crimes are committed, and other innumerable sins, by which the King of Kings is justly provoked to anger.

Where is thy prudence? where thy judgment? But I do not speak in this manner as if I supposed, that it was unlawful for Christians to enter into war for the defence of their cities. I know that just wars are allowed, not only by the holy Fathers,[1] but also by the precursor of Our Lord *"greater than whom hath not arisen amongst those born of woman"*

He said to the soldiers not that they should desert their service as being unlawful, but that, being content with their pay, they should *"do violence to no man"* (St. Luke, iii. 14) In my *"Controversies"* I have also defended just wars. I do not therefore speak against war simply in itself; but I exhort you to follow that which is more perfect, and often more useful, according to what St. Paul says to the Corinthians: *"Already indeed there is plainly a fault among you, that you have lawsuits one with another. Why do you not rather hate wrong? Why do you not rather suffer yourselves to be defrauded?"* (1 Epist. to Corinthians v. 7.) And St. James adds in his Epistle: *"From whence are wars and contentions among you? Are they not hence from your concupiscence? You covet, and have not: you kill, and envy, and cannot obtain. You contend and war, and have not, because you ask not."* (chap, iv.) Whoever earnestly aspires after the kingdom of heaven, would not easily be moved to war by the loss of one city; but he would seek after those who could settle the dispute without expense and danger. But let us proceed to other points.

THE INHABITANTS OF THE KINGDOM OF GOD.

THE kingdom of heaven is called a "Habitation" because it contains such a multitude of different inhabitants; no palace or city, but only large kingdoms contain such numbers. There, as St. Paul tells us in his Epistle to the Hebrews, are many thousands of angels; there also are " the spirits of the Just made perfect," to whom belong all who have departed in the Lord from Abel, even to the last good man that will die at the end of the world. But not only will the souls of the Just be there, but also their glorious bodies, each of which shall shine like the sun in the kingdom of their Father, as our Lord assures us in St. Matthew.

With regard to the angels, we who live on this earth scarcely know anything of them but their names.[1] We learn from the vision of the prophet Isaias, (chap, vi.) that some are called Seraphim, and others Cherubim [2] some Thrones, others Dominations: some Principalities, others Powers, as St. Paul mentions in his Epistle to the Colossians: (chap. i. ver. 16.) in his Epistle to the Ephesians he also speaks of **"Virtues,"** and in another place, **Archangels** are spoken of: Angels are finally ranked amongst them, of whom there is so frequent mention throughout the Holy Scriptures. From these nine names, it is the unanimous opinion of learned doctors, that there are ***nine "orders" of angels***, each of which contains many thousands, according to the prophet Daniel: ***"Thousands of thousands ministered to him, and ten thousand times a hundred thousand stood before him."*** (chap. vii. 10.) And Job asks: " Is there any numbering of his soldiers?"

But although all the angels are doubtless most happy, and wonderfully resplendent with the glory of every divine gift, yet those are called *" Seraphim"* who burn with the flames of love: the others *" Cherubim"* who shine with the splendour of knowledge: those are named " Thrones" who enjoy an inexpressible tranquillity in the divine contemplation: those "Dominations" who rule this lower world, as the ministers of a mighty commander: others "Powers," because they do signs and wonders by the command of their Almighty Lord: others " Principalities," because they have power over the kings and princes of the world: some again are named "Archangels," because they assist the prelates of the Church: and many, in fine, are called " Angels," since they are the guardians and protectors of all that live upon the earth.

But these are not the only significations of the names of the angels:[3] " they are also images or representations of the greatness of God: thus the seraphim, by their burning love, represent as it were in a glass, the infinite love of God which alone induced Him to create the angels, man, and all other creatures, whom He still preserves. The cherubim in like manner represent the infinite wisdom of God, which hath regulated all things by number, weight, and measure. The thrones also, by a perfect image as it were, show us that profound *" rest"* which God enjoys on His throne; who, whilst all things are in motion, remains unalterable, tranquilly ruling and directing events.

The dominations too tell us, that it is God who alone truly rules all things, because He alone can either preserve them, or annihilate them. The virtues convince us, that it is God "who alone doth wonderful things" and who hath reserved to himself alone to renew signs, and to multiply wonders. The powers signify by their name, that God alone is absolutely and truly powerful, to whom nothing is impossible, because in Him alone true power resides.

The principalities signify, that God is the Prince over the kings of the earth, the King of kings, and Lord of lords. The archangels signify, that God is the true High Priest of all the churches. The angels, that God is the true Father of orphans; and that although He hath given His angels to be our guardians, He himself is present with each one, to guard and protect him. The prophet who has said, ***"He hath given his angels charge over thee, to keep thee in all thy ways," introduces the Almighty thus speaking: "I am with him in tribulation, I will deliver him, and I will glorify him."*** (Psalm xc.) And our Lord, who had said, ***"their angels in heaven always see the face of my Father who is in heaven" has also added: "Are not two sparrows sold for a farthing; and not one of them shall fall upon the ground without your Father. But the very hairs of your head are all numbered. Fear not therefore; better are you than many sparrows."*** (St. Matthew, chap. x. 29, &c.) Such are the few points that we know about the angels, concerning whom you may read St. Bernard on ***"Consideration"*** (Lib. v.) from whom I have taken these details.

With these nine orders of the angels, correspond on the other hand that multitude of holy men, which no one can number, as we learn from the Apocalypse. This multitude contains also nine "orders ;" for some are patriarchs, some prophets, some apostles, some martyrs and confessors; whilst others are pastors, doctors, priests, Levites, monks, and hermits, holy women, virgins, widows, or married people. Wherefore, my soul, I beseech thee to consider what great happiness it will be, to be united with such great saints!

St. Jerome mentions,(Epistola ad Paulinum) that he visited many provinces, and many people, and crossed many seas, that he might see and hear those celebrated men, whom he had known by their works. Queen of Saba came from the ends of the earth to hear the wisdom of Solomon; and to St. Antony, the hermit, men hastened from all parts, being moved by the fame of his sanctity: even Emperors themselves courted his friendship.

But what will it be to behold hereafter so many angels, so many just men, to be united with them in the closest friendship, and to be made partakers of their happiness? Were we to behold, in this our exile, one angel arrayed in all his beauty, who would not eagerly wish to meet him? What therefore must it be, to behold all the angels in one place? And if only one of the prophets, apostles, or doctors of the Church were to descend from heaven, with what curiosity and attention would he be heard! Now in the kingdom of God, we shall be allowed to behold not one only, but all the prophets, apostles, and doctors, with whom we shall continually hold sweet converse. How greatly does the sun rejoice the whole earth: but what will be the glory from innumerable Suns in the kingdom of God, all animate, intelligent, and exulting in their joy! This union with the angels and men, all of whom are most wise and excellent, appears to me so delightful, that I consider it alone will be a great happiness, and on this account, would willingly be deprived of all the pleasures of this life.

THE MONARCHICAL FORM
OF THE KINGDOM OF GOD.

THE third reason why it is called a "Kingdom" is, because there alone is to be found a perfect form of government. There is this difference between a kingdom and a republic: in the former the supreme power is possessed by one person: in the latter it is divided amongst many. But in the kingdoms of this world, supreme power in the true and proper sense of the word, cannot exist. For although a king, without the advice or consent of others, can command something to be done; yet it cannot be accomplished without the approbation of his subjects.

It even often happens that he cannot give a command, or at least will not dare to do so, should all his subjects be against him. How many great kings and emperors have there been, who were either deserted by their army, or put to death!

History is full of such examples. Supreme power therefore is useless to the kings of this world, because they can never execute any thing, unless their subjects approve of it. But the power of God, who is truly and essentially King of kings, dependeth upon no one, but

His own will: and since He is omnipotent, He can do all things; neither doth He stand in need of soldiers, arms, or any external aid. And when He makes use of the ministration of angels, men, or even inanimate things, He does so because He wills, not because he requires them. For He who without any assistance made heaven and earth, and all things therein, by His only word, and who preserves them by His will, can also govern them by His power alone.

But God reigns in the truest sense of the word, not only because He possesses supreme power; but also because He alone knows how to govern: He stands not in need of any council, or ministers of state. ***Who hath known the mind of the Lord? or who hath been his counsellor?" says St. Paul:*** and before him the prophet Isaias: ***"Who hath forwarded the Spirit of the Lord? or who hath been his counsellor, and hath taught him? With whom hath he consulted, and who hath instructed him, and taught him the path of justice, and taught him knowledge, and showed him the way of understanding?"*** (chap. xl. 13, 14;)

Wherefore a monarchy, which is the best form of government, is to be found in God alone in its true and perfect nature. He is not only ***" terrible over all the kingdoms of the earth,"*** as it is said in the Psalms; but He is also ***" King above all gods,"*** as it is expressed in another place. Others are false gods or rather devils, according the prophet: ***"All the gods of the Gentiles are devils."*** (Psalm xcv.) Some are gods by participation, as the kings of the earth and the angels of heaven, thus ***" I have said: You are gods and all of you the sons of the Most High."*** (Psalm lxxxi.)

But all these gods are under the power of that God, who reigneth in heaven: He alone then is truly a great king. This Nabuchodonosor, king of Babylon, acknowledged in these words, after he had suffered a most severe punishment for his pride: ***"Now at the end of the days,***

I Nabuchodonosor lifted up my eyes to heaven, and my sense was restored to me: and I blessed the most High, and I praised and glorified Him that liveth for ever: for his kingdom is an everlasting power, and his kingdom is to all generations. And all the inhabitants of the earth are reputed as nothing before him: for He doth according to his will, as well with the powers of heaven, as among the inhabitants of the earth: and there is none that can resist His hand, and say to him: Why hast thou done it?" (Daniel, chap. iv. 31, &c.) Thus he spoke, giving us all an example to humble ourselves under the powerful hand of God, as St. Peter admonishes us: and to be more delighted with serving the King of kings, that we may experience His goodness, than proudly to resist His will, lest we be forced to feel the weight of His avenging hand.

ALL THE BLESSED ARE KINGS.

THE fourth reason[1] why heaven is called a kingdom is because all the Blessed in heaven are kings, and all the conditions of being such most aptly apply to them. For although the saints in heaven serve God, as it is mentioned in the Apocalypse, yet at the same time they reign also; for in the same book, and in the same chapter, where it is said, *" His servants shall serve Him," a little lower we are told that " They shall reign for ever and ever."* (chap, xxii.) But all the Blessed will not only serve and reign at the same time; they will also be called servants and sons. Thus God speaks in the Apocalypse: *"He that shall overcome shall possess these things, and I will be his God, and he shall be my son."* (chap. xxi. 7.)

Wherefore, as they can be both servants and sons, so also they can be both servants and kings; they are servants because they were created by God, to whom they owe obedience, and from whom they receive their being, and all things else; and David makes no exception when he says: *"All creatures serve him."* They are also the sons of God, since they were born of God by water and the Holy Spirit; they are kings, too, because they have received the dignity from the King of kings, who is called by this name in the Apocalypse, " King of kings, and Lord of lords." (chap. xix. 16.)

But it may perhaps be said, that it is not difficult for one to be both a king of the earth, and a servant of God, for thus the Psalmist speaks: ***And now, ye kings, understand, receive instruction, you that judge the earth. Serve ye the Lord with fear: and rejoice unto him with trembling.*** " (Ps. ii.) But to be a king in the kingdom of heaven, and a servant of the King of heaven who can understand or comprehend this? And yet such is the truth, which faith believes and understands. The just, therefore, will also be kings in the kingdom of heaven, because they will be made partakers of the royal dignity, and power, and riches, &c., of that kingdom. This is what the Holy Spirit clearly teaches us, especially in three passages from the Scripture; the first of which occurs in St. Matthew: ***Blessed are the poor in spirit, for theirs is the kingdom of heaven*** *" (chap, v.) In another part: " Come, ye blessed of my Father, possess you the kingdom prepared for you from the foundation of the world." (St. Matthew, chap, xxv.) The third passage is from the Apocalypse: To him that shall overcome I will give to sit with me on my throne: as I also have overcome, and have sat down with my Father in His throne." (chap, iii.)*

What can be clearer than these words? The kingdom of heaven is promised the possession of it will be given to us at the last day we shall have a seat on the royal throne of the Son of God, and of His Father, our eternal King: what is this but a participation of the same kingdom, which God possesses from eternity? St. Paul also adds his testimony: *"If we suffer, we shall reign with Him;" and St. John likewise, in the beginning of the Apocalypse: "I, John, your brother, and your partner in tribulation, and in the kingdom," &c.* And

St. James, in his Epistle: ***"Hath not God chosen the poor in this world, rich in faith, and heirs of the kingdom which God hath promised to them that love Him?"*** (chap. ii. 5.) But the kingdom of heaven is not lessened, because it is divided amongst innumerable angels and men. This kingdom is not like the kingdoms of the world, which cannot well be divided; but should they be distributed into parts, the division weakens them, and at length they are destroyed. But not so with the kingdom above, which is perfectly possessed by all, and wholly by each one, just as the sun is seen by all and each of the inhabitants of earth, whom it equally enlightens and vivifies. But this point will be more easily understood when we explain the good things that are to be found in the kingdom of heaven.

We must now dwell on the conditions or qualities which are required in kings, so that we may be convinced the saints and blessed spirits can justly be called the Kings of the kingdom of heaven.

There are two qualities especially necessary for kings -wisdom and justice. But with wisdom the Scripture joins prudence and counsel, and all other things that relate to intelligence; with justice are united mercy, clemency, and other virtues that adorn and perfect the will. Wisdom, therefore, is required that the king may have knowledge; justice, that he may govern his subjects with equity. On this account, Solomon, in the beginning of his reign, being admonished by God to ask for what he wished, asked for wisdom, which is the chief of all the virtues required in kings.

His petition was acceptable before God, as we read in the third Book of Kings, and therefore he obtained what he prayed for. Would that he had asked for justice also: perhaps he would not then have fallen into so many crimes. But more justly does David speak in that psalm, where he prays for blessings on Solomon his son: ***"Give to the king thy judgment, God; and to the king's son*** *thy justice."* (Psalm lxxi.) From these words it appears that he foresaw Solomon would ask for wisdom, and therefore David prayed that "justice and judgment" might be given to him, which without wisdom cannot exist, although wisdom, though but imperfectly, may exist without justice. The Book of Wisdom, which was written for the instruction of kings, thus speaks: ***Love justice, you that are judges of the earth." (chap, i.) It commences from "justice," because it is not only in itself necessary for kings, but also because it disposes us to receive wisdom. Thus, a little lower, it adds: "For wisdom will not enter into a malicious soul, nor dwell in a body subject to sin." In fine, Jeremias, foretelling the virtues of Christ, the eternal King says: " Behold, the days come, saith the Lord, and I will raise up to David a just branch: and a king shall reign and be wise, and shall execute judgment and justice in the earth." (chap, xxiii. 5.) Truly, therefore, are "wisdom and justice required in kings."***

Now every one must acknowledge, that all the blessed in heaven, though they may have been whilst on earth simple and ignorant, are now possessed of the deepest wisdom, and so eminently endowed with the virtue of justice, that they might justly become kings of any kingdom. For all the blessed behold the very essence of God Himself, which is the ***"first cause"*** of all things; and thereby, from this fountain of uncreated wisdom, they drink in such wisdom as neither Solomon nor any other mortal possessed, except our Lord Jesus Christ, who, even during the time of His mortal life, saw God, for in Him ***"were hid all the treasures of wisdom and knowledge. "*** But, besides the wisdom which the blessed possess, there is also given to them a full measure of justice, so that they can never sin, nor even wish to sin; thus St. Augustine speak: (Liber de Correptione et Gratiâ, cap. 12.) The first liberty of the Will was, to be able not to commit sin, but the last will be much greater, not to be able to sin." But he who cannot commit sin, cannot be unjust; and since perfect charity is the same as perfect justice, as St. Augustine asserts,(Lib. de Naturâ et Gratiâ, (cap. ult.)) he who loves not God with the greatest and most perfect love, cannot possess the perfect justice. Now, they who behold God that infinite and pure Being cannot certainly turn away from Him, but they must ever love Him with the most ardent love; whence it follows, that all the saints in heaven are perfectly wise, perfectly just, and therefore most proper to reign.

Arise then, my soul, and as far as possible consider, what happiness it will be to reign with God! And thus - to omit other considerations penetrate heaven itself on the wings of contemplation, and behold that glorious throne of which our Saviour speaks: ***"To him that shall overcome, I will give to sit with me on my throne, as I also have overcome, and have sat down with my Father in His throne."***(Apoc. chap. iii, 21.) How great will the glory be for that just soul to be placed with such an infinite multitude of angels, on the very throne of Christ and of God! And by His just judgment to be proclaimed a conqueror over the world, and the rulers thereof, and all invisible powers!

And how will this soul exult with gladness, when, delivered from every toil and danger, she shall behold herself gloriously triumphant over all her enemies! What more will she desire, when she shall be made a partaker of all the gifts of her Lord, even of a participation of His throne and Kingdom? Oh, how zealously do they fight on earth, and with what patience do they bear all things for the love of Christ, who, with a lively faith and a sure hope, contemplate such divine honours in heaven!

THE HAPPINESS ENJOYED
IN THE KINGDOM OF GOD.

THE fifth reason, it appears to me, why heaven is called a kingdom is, because the good things enjoyed by the blessed seem something like those possessed by the kings of the earth; but they are so much greater and more excellent as heaven is superior to earth. Wherefore, the kingdom that is prepared for the blessed is not simply called a " kingdom" but the "kingdom of heaven," that so we may understand the difference between the pleasures of each the one being limited, base, mean, and temporal; whilst the others are boundless, noble, spiritual, and above all, eternal.

The goods of an earthly kingdom are considered to be, power, honour, riches, and pleasures. An earthly monarch can command his subjects; and if they obey him not, he can imprison them, banish them, fine them, scourge them, or put them to death. Hence kings are feared by the people, for they appear, as it were, to be gods. Again, kings wish to be honoured with almost a supernatural veneration, by the knee being bent before them, as if in adoration; and often they will not deign to listen to us, unless we bow down to the earth; and whenever they appear in public, they wish every one to make way for them. In addition to this, they require a large "exchequer," full of gold and silver; neither do they count their money by hundreds or thousands of pounds, but by ten hundred thousands; and with reason, since they are obliged to support, not ten or twenty servants, but to lead whole armies forth against their enemies.

Lastly, they do not condescend to indulge in ordinary amusements, but only in those which they suppose become their royal majesty such as banquets, hunting, and the theatre on which they squander immense sums of money. Now these are the chief pleasures which earthly princes possess; and all of them are short and fading, since they begin with life, and end in death; unless it should sometime happen, that their life was of longer continuance than their kingdom.

But, moreover, these pleasures are not pure, because power is joined with infirmity, honour with ignominy, riches with poverty, and joy with sorrow and affliction. The power of a prince is such, that the people should depend on the will of their prince; but power is infirm, because the prince depends on the strength and resources of his people. What can a king do in capturing or defending a city, if the people are either unwilling or unable to assist him? But a prince depends not only on the resources of his subjects, but also on walls, fortifications, arms, engines of war, and "money" which is called the nerves of war. Wherefore the people depend on the pleasure of their prince, and serve him alone; the prince, on the contrary, depends on many men and many things, all of which he is obliged to employ.

In fine, a king can imprison, banish, or put to death his subjects; but a king also [1] can be imprisoned, banished, &c. Julius Cæsar, Caius, Nero, Galba, Vitellius, Domitian, Commodus, Heliogabalus, &c., afford examples of this truth. And not only these who were so wicked, but also those of much milder dispositions, such as Alexander, Mammæas, Grordianus the younger, Pertinax, Tacitus, Numerianus, Probus, Gratian, Valentinian the second, not to mention St. Edward the Confessor, St. Wenceslaus, king of Bohemia, St. Sigismund, king of Burgundy, St. Canute, king of Denmark, &c. Let us now speak of their honours.

Whilst kings are present before others, they are certainly honoured and respected; but when absent, they are often ridiculed and spoken against: even when present, many praise them with their lips, whilst they despise them with their heart, so that, if the number of those that praise them and those that revile them could be counted, the latter would be found more numerous than the former. Truly, therefore, the ignominy of kings is often greater than their glory, since few are those who honour their dignity when present, but many accuse them when absent of avarice, and others of cruelty, others of luxury, &c.

But perhaps the riches of kings are pure, without any admixture of poverty. No, for none are so poor as kings; they have immense incomes and great treasures, but their debts and expenses are much greater.

He that possesseth little is not so poor as one who desireth many things, because he stands in need of them. And is it not a great proof of poverty when kings beg a mite, as it were, from the poor themselves, by exacting as taxes what is necessary for their support? I do not speak thus as if I wished to blame the exaction of tributes, for I know it is just they should be paid to kings, according to what St. Paul says in his Epistle to the Romans: ***"Wherefore be subject not only for wrath, but also for conscience' sake. For therefore, also, you pay tribute. For they are the ministers of God, serving unto this purpose. Render therefore to all men their dues. Tribute, to whom tribute is due: custom, to whom custom: fear, to whom fear: honour, to whom honour."*** (chap, xiii:7) But I merely wished to show the miserable condition of kings, who, although they abound in riches, are yet compelled to collect a part of them from the poor and destitute. But what shall we say of their pleasures?

Kings have certainly gardens, orchards, sumptuous banquets, hunting, &c., and whatever else can amuse them; but they also have the gout, headaches, complaints in the liver; and what is more distressing, the most painful cares of the mind, which deprive them whole nights of sleep, together with suspicions, fears, and anguish. If the doors of their chambers creak at night, they suspect treachery; if an armed multitude have been seen, a desertion is apprehended.

Thus, joy is mixed with sorrow, and rest interrupted by care; this is the reason why many have resigned their crown, that they might lead a private life. But let us hear how St. John Chrysostom, in one of his Homilies (Hom. 66) to the people of Antioch, speaks of the kings of his time: " Look not at the diadem, but at the multitude of cares look not at the purple, but at the soul, blacker than the purple itself. The crown does not so much circle the head, as cares do the soul.

Neither consider the troops of attendants, but the multitude of troubles. For no private house can be found so full of cares as a palace: everyday deaths are expected, but in the night one cannot tell how often the soul is terrified, and thinks it is about to depart. And all this in time of peace. But when a war breaks out, what can be more miserable than life? How many dangers befall friends and subjects!

The royal pavement is always sprinkled with the blood of relations. If you wish me to relate some facts, you will perhaps acknowledge them. I will tell you some that happened in our own time. One king having suspected his wife of adultery already the mother of many kings, bound her naked, and delivered her to the beasts of the mountain. What a life do you suppose he must have led? He would not surely have taken such a terrible revenge, unless he had been consumed by some disease. This same person murdered his own son also, but being seized, he destroyed himself. After this, another was taken away by poison; and his son, although he had done no injury, was deprived of his sight for fear of the future consequences. Another [2] ended his life very miserably; he was burned to death with his chariots and horses, &c. No one can express the sorrows he was obliged to endure, when he came to the throne.

And the present king who now rules, when he was crowned with the diadem, did he not begin to be surrounded with toil, danger, sorrow, and treachery? But such is not the state of the kingdom of heaven." [3] How truly this great saint hath said, "Such is not the state of the kingdom of heaven" we shall now see.

The kings of the kingdom of heaven, who all live in happiness with God, possess power without infirmity, honour without ignominy, riches without poverty, pleasure without pain; for of them the Psalmist speaks: "***There shall no evil come to thee: nor shall the scourge come near thy dwelling.***" (Psalm xc.10)

And in the Apocalypse: "***God shall wipe away all tears from their eyes; and death shall be no more, nor mourning, nor crying, nor sorrow shall be any more, for the former things are passed away.***" [4] (ch. xxi. 4.)

Wherefore exceeding great is the power of these heavenly kings, without the least admixture of infirmity. One angel, without an army, without swords and spears, instantly slew one hundred and eighty-five thousand Assyrians; neither was he afraid of being wounded by any of the soldiers. St. Gregory relates in his ***"Dialogues"***(Lib. iii. cap. 36) ***that a certain holy man, when the executor with uplifted arm was about to behead him, exclaimed, "St. John, save me !" and immediately the executioner could neither move nor*** *stir his hand in anyway. St. John therefore heard the prayer of his client; and with such quickness was the executioner struck, that the stroke, though just falling, was prevented.*

Such then is the power of the kings of heaven, that neither the distance of place, nor the situation in which this just but defenceless man was placed, nor the multitude of armed enemies, could prevent St. John from delivering him from instant death. Numerous examples of the like nature could be mentioned.

The honour these heavenly kings possess is so great, that not only good men, but the wicked also, and even devils, are forced to respect them. Many there are who despised and spurned these holy men whilst they were upon earth; but afterwards they honoured and venerated them when translated to heaven, especially if the Church by a public decree numbered them among the saints: and even the demons themselves, who were wont to harass the saints with temptations when living in the flesh; and even, by the permission of God, to beat them with many stripes, now fear their relics and images since they reign with God. What shall I say of the riches these kings enjoy? *"Their great treasure is, to want nothing, because God is all in all. He is not rich who possesseth many things; but he who desireth nothing, because he standeth in need of nothing: the soul ought to be rich, but not the coffers; heaven and earth and all things therein, contribute to the riches of the saints, for what do not they possess who are "heirs of God, and joint-heirs with Christ?" and whom the Father hath appointed " heirs of all things ?"*

There now remain but the pleasures which the blessed enjoy in heaven: these are pure and sweet, without any ingredient of sorrow or affliction: we have already heard from the Apocalypse, that God will wipe away all tears from their eyes, and that sorrow and mourning will be no more. But on this point we shall dwell more at length, when we speak of Paradise. We have now seen, that the good things which the blessed and all the saints will enjoy in heaven together, are such, that they can in no way be compared with the pleasures of earth; especially since the latter are temporary, the former eternal.

WHAT IMPORTANCE MEN ATTACH TO EARTHLY KINGDOMS, AND WHAT IMPORTANCE OUGHT TO BE ATTACHED TO THE KINGDOM OF HEAVEN.

LET us now consider with what eagerness men seek after earthly kingdoms; though insignificant, frail, and full of care and trouble, that hereby we may be convinced with what ardour our heavenly Kingdom ought to be desired and sought after. The passion for dominion, without doubt far exceeds all other passions; for a kingdom is not one individual "good but a collection of all those pleasures which are so much prized by men. These are, power, honour, riches, and delights, as we have already seen; there is the liberty of living just as we please, which is naturally pleasing not only to man, but also to beasts; there is excellence, and a kind of divinity as it were, on account of which kings have no equals in their government, but are superior to all, above all, and are reverenced by all.

Hence it is, that when kings wish to make a promise, they can find nothing greater than half of their kingdom. Thus Assuerus addressed Esther: ***"What wilt thou, Esther? What is thy request? If thou should even ask one half of the kingdom, it shall be given thee."*** (Esther v. 3.) And Herod said to Herodias: ***"Whatsoever*** *thou shalt ask I will give it thee, though it be the half of my kingdom."*

Hence it is, that to possess or extend kingdoms, men consider it lawful to throw aside every right; nor is there anything so sacred which they will not violate for the sake of reigning. The very first individual who unjustly waged war against his friends and neighbours, was Ninus: he broke through every law, just and unjust, that he might enlarge his kingdom, as St. Augustine (De Civitate Dei, Lib. iv. cap. 6) testifies. Julius Caesar was the first to oppress his country, which he did for the sake of being emperor. Maximinus the Thracian slew Alexander by his soldiers, that he might succeed to the empire, although he had received from him many and great benefits. Philip the Arabian did the same also to Gordian the emperor. But the lust of reigning arms man, not only against neighbours and benefactors, but also against brothers, nephews, and even fathers. Thus Romulus killed his brother Remus, and Caracalla his brother Geta. Athalia slew all the children of Ochozias her son, who was king, that so she might obtain the crown.

Thus the desires of sovereignty impels not only men, but also females to commit the most shocking crimes. Sinochus, a Persian, contrived to murder his father and brother, in order that he alone might reign. But why do I mention these instances? the mother of Nero, when the astrologer told her that her son would be emperor, but that she would be destroyed by him, is reported to have exclaimed, "Let him destroy me, provided he may reign !" Wherefore, this ambitious woman considered the kingdom to be of such importance to her son, that she preferred it to her own life. But this thirst for ruling not only makes injustice, to be justice, and arms man against a Brother, nephew, and parent, but it also violates the sacred obligation of an oath, [1] when a throne is in view. If we are to give credit to Cicero (De Officiis, Lib. iii.) we are told that Julius Cæsar was always accustomed to repeat these words of Euripides: *"**If an oath is to be violated, it may be violated for the sake of reigning: in other matters, cultivate piety.**"*

I omit innumerable other examples which demonstrate to all ages, that nothing whatever is prized more by men than a kingdom.; and yet, not only do kings reign but for a short period, but also every kingdom will quickly be utterly destroyed; whilst the kingdom of the blessed shall alone remain for ever. Hear the prophet Daniel: *"**But in the days of those kingdoms, the God of heaven will set up a kingdom that shall never be destroyed, and his kingdom shall not be delivered up to another people; and it shall break in pieces, and shall consume all these kingdoms, and itself shall stand for ever.**"* (ch. ii. 44.) This prophecy will be fulfilled at the end of the world; for then not only all great monarchies, but also small states, cities, and all the temporal power of princes will vanish away; but the kingdom of Christ and his saints will be eternal, according to the words of St. Luke: *"**And of His kingdom there is no end.**"*

Now if an earthly kingdom, which passeth quickly away, and which is obtained but by few, and full of many sorrows, be so ardently loved, sought after, preferred before every thing else, and acquired only by great dangers and bloodshed: why do so few love their heavenly kingdom, and so negligently seek after it? And yet, if the Holy Scriptures are to be believed, we are certain that this kingdom is open to all men, can be possessed without the effusion of blood, and is without any comparison superior to all earthly kingdoms.

If I should say, Despise this kingdom that you may obtain a small farm or a vineyard, you would justly be astonished and laugh at me: but when I say, or rather when God says, Despise this vile and contemptible kingdom, and seek that which is noble and great, [2] why do you not desire it, and hasten to obtain it? I do not know what answer to make, except that the glory of this earthly kingdom is always before our eyes, and is touched, as it were, with our hands; whilst our heavenly kingdom can neither be seen, nor touched, nor even conceived by faith. This, indeed, is true; but if we attentively consider what force the authenticity, truth, and inspiration of Scripture carry with them, and how forcibly and clearly this same Scripture speaks on this point, which is confirmed by the powerful testimony of many ages, not only by miracles but also by blood, we shall certainly exclaim: ***"Thy testimonies, Lord, are become exceedingly credible."(Ps. xcii.)***

The obscurity of our faith, therefore, is not the reason why we are not inflamed with a desire for this heavenly kingdom. But being occupied by exterior things, and weighed down by the force of custom, we have no time to think and consider what is expedient for us. We do not follow the advice of our Lord, by entering into our chamber and shutting the door of our heart; we do not earnestly beseech God to direct us in so important an affair. But if, throwing aside for a time all minor cares, we were seriously to think on the kingdom of heaven; how easily and securely it can be acquired. And what an ^immense difference there is between things temporal and things eternal between that which is most insignificant and that which is most excellent between what is of very little importance and what is of the utmost importance; in fine, between an earthly kingdom and a heavenly kingdom. Did we, I repeat, consider these truths, doubtless we should have such a contempt for all earthly thrones, crowns, and sceptres; and, on the other hand, such an ardour for the heavenly things would rise in us, that, so far from being difficult, it would be a most easy task for us to employ all our strength in seeking and acquiring the kingdom of God, for which, as our true and last end, we were made by our wise Creator.[3]

THE FIRST MEANS OF ATTAINING TO THE KINGDOM OF GOD.

LET us now consider what is necessary to be done, in order that we may possess this most blessed and happy kingdom. But we need not say much on this point, since the King of heaven himself came upon earth to teach us; and thus, as our Master and Leader, he has pointed out to us four most excellent and secure means. The first is: "Seek first the kingdom of God and his justice, and all these things shall be added unto you" Our end is the kingdom of God, which kingdom will be given to us if we arrive there by the way pointed out to us by our Leader. Now, the ***"justice"*** of this kingdom is the mark at which we ought to aim, if we wish to gain the reward. For Cassian, in his first " Colloquy," teaches the end is one thing and the mark an-other; the mark is the sign to which the arrows are di-rected, the end is the reward which those receive who reach that mark. Now, the mark proposed by God for our actions is "justice," and the reward the kingdom of heaven. But the justice of God is not the justice of the Scribes and the Pharisees, which consisted merely in the external observance of the law; nor is it the justice of the philosophers, which, corrupted by sin, did not extend beyond the light of reason.

But it is the justice of the Gospel which teaches us, *"to love God with our whole heart, with our whole soul, with our whole strength, and our neighbour (though our enemy) as ourselves." Of this end St. Paul speaks: " You have your fruit unto sanctification, and the end life everlasting." (Romans, chap. vi. 22.)*

This is the lesson, therefore, which our Master teaches us, "First of all to seek the kingdom of God and His justice:" that is, our chief concern and only desire should be directed, not towards temporal goods, but to obtain the kingdom of heaven, by a perfect and most diligent observance of this first and greatest commandment. But because few do this, therefore *" many are called, but few are chosen;"* for many live in such a manner that the kingdom of heaven is but a secondary consideration with them, and the justice of God an indifferent object, as if our Lord had said, "Seek first the kingdom of this world and its pleasures, and the kingdom of God shall be added unto you." But not so insignificant is the kingdom of God, that it should be forced or those who prefer everything else to its possession.

But if we wish to learn an easy way to obtain the justice of God, which most truly and certainly leads to this kingdom, let us hear Christ, our Teacher: *"Blessed are they that hunger and thirst after justice, for they shall have their fill."* Is it then, O Lord, so easy to find justice with thee, that it is sufficient only to hunger and thirst" after it? Truly blessed would all the poor be, if, merely by being hungry and thirsty after money, they could be so filled with it as to desire nothing more. But one is quite different from the other. For they who hunger sad. thirst after justice that is, they who seek justice as anxiously and as eagerly as those who suffer from thirst and desire water, or from hunger and desire food these always think of justice, they aspire after it and what is far better, they ask it of God with many and unceasing tears.

Such petitions God always listens to with joy; and He so falls them with the riches of His justice, that, being satiated thereby, they produce the words and the works of justice. But money is not such a good that he who desires it, or asks it of God, is immediately heard; for many abuse their riches, but justice no one can abuse. In fine, justice is like wisdom, of which St. James speaks: *" If any of you want wisdom, let him ask of God, who giveth to all men abundantly, and upbraideth not: and it shall be given him"*. Unspeakable clemency of our Lord, who more easily and willingly grants what is necessary for us, than we ask or desire it from Him! It, therefore, we stand in need of the wisdom of the saints, or of the gifts of justice, both of which are necessary for us to obtain the kingdom of heaven, let us ask them of God from our heart, seriously, with sighs and tears, and we shall surely obtain them.

God giveth to all that ask in this manner; nor doth He repel any one, or give covetously or moderately, but bountifully: neither doth He rebuke us, as if He were angry that we besought Him so often. What can we say, then? Who can bring excuse for his ignorance or infirmity in the day of judgment? Seek only after justice, and ask it of God, and thou shalt be so filled that no more wilt thou desire the delights of the flesh, nor the allurements of honours, or of any other earthly good; but thou wilt live in this world so justly, soberly, and piously, as to arrive in the next at an eternal kingdom.

THE SECOND MEANS OF ATTAINING TO THE KINGDOM OF GOD.

ANOTHER road, which our Leader has pointed out to us is this: "Blessed are the poor in spirit, for theirs is the kingdom of heaven." Here we are not commanded to keep our coffers entirely empty, but our heart and affections free from the desire of external things. Our Lord offers to us immense treasures, but He will not give them, unless we offer Him our heart completely disengaged from creatures. *" The desire of money is the root of all evils"*(1 Tim. vi. 10.) In Greek it is called φιλαργυρια that is, the love of money. But the root of all good is charity, and these two can never remain together. Wherefore, unless we truly and perfectly become "poor in spirit," so that we are neither affected by riches nor by poverty, and unless we readily give something to the poor, and do not convert it to our own use, except through necessity, we cannot obtain the justice of the kingdom of God, and, consequently, we cannot enter heaven. This is the true way that leadeth to life eternal; upon this road our Saviour Himself was the first to enter, *"Who being rich, became poor for your*

sakes, that through His poverty you might be rich." (2 Epist. to Cor. chap. viii. 9.)

And although He kept a purse, yet He entrusted it to Judas, who He knew to be a thief, that so we might comprehend how free His soul was from the love of money. "Upon this path the Apostles also entered, though it would not have been difficult for them to have enriched themselves, since they were renowned for signs and wonders, and spoke the languages of many nations, and were admired by the whole world for their wisdom. But they who had once spoke the words, Behold we have left all things, and have followed thee;" who had tasted how sweet it was to be free from the love of money, having food and wherewith to be covered, they considered virtue and the justice of God to be their great gain. On this road also walked, not only monks and hermits, but even kings and pontiffs who have thus arrived at the kingdom of heaven.

St. Lewis, King of France, was certainly rich; but because he was at the same time poor in spirit, he used common garments, fasted frequently, was liberal to the poor, and severe to himself alone: he did not spend his money in banquets and pageants. St. Gregory also, who was a Pope, possessed many and large estates belonging to the Church; but Because he likewise was ***"poor in spirit"*** he was so liberal with his alms, though parsimonious in his own regard, that he seemed to exceed the bounds of liberality towards others, and of neglect towards himself and his friends. But this is the way that leadeth to life.

St. Paula, a Roman lady, whose life is written by St. Jerome,[1] was amongst women as poor in spirit, as she was rich in wealth. Though of most noble descent, she spent her money in erecting monasteries, and supporting the poor with such liberality, that it seemed to be her desire to be reduced to such poverty, as to compel others of their charity, to defray her funeral expenses.

And how much she mortified her own body, we may be convinced by the fact, that she abstained from flesh, eggs, and wine; for a linen garment, she wore sackcloth; she slept on the bare ground, and with frequent prayers and tears, endeavoured to wash away even her trifling faults.

St. Hedwiges [2] also, Queen of Poland, though rich in worldly goods, was richer by her poverty of spirit, being content with only one mean garment, which she wore even in the depth of winter; she fasted daily, Sundays and great festivals being excepted; and with stripes,, watchings, and all kinds of mortifications, she thus subdued her body. From these circumstances we may learn to what purposes she applied her riches, and what little affection, if any at all, she had towards them. It is not then wonderful, that this woman arrived so quickly at the kingdom of heaven, being so poor in spirit, and so free from all other cares.

THE THIRD MEANS OF ATTAINING THE KINGDOM OF GOD.

THE third way pointed out by our Leader is this: *" Blessed are they that suffer persecution for justice sake; for theirs is the kingdom of heaven" (St. Matthew, ch. v. 10.)* Truly admirable is the doctrine of Christ our teacher, which however is hidden from the "wise" of this world. For who would have believed, unless God had said it, that it is a blessed thing to be poor, but rich in afflictions? And yet truly hath He spoken. Nothing is more calculated to acquire the true riches which merit the kingdom of heaven, than a mind free from all affection to money, and at the same time full of a desire to suffer for Christ. Hear our Lord in St. Luke: *" Woe to you that are filled; woe to you that are rich, for you have your consolation; woe to you that laugh? (chap, vi.)* And again in the same place: *" Blessed are ye that hunger now, for ye shall be filled. Blessed are ye that weep now, for ye shall laugh. Blessed shall ye be when men shall hate you, and when they shall separate you, and shall reproach you, and cast out your name as evil, for the*

***Son of man's sake. Be glad in that day and rejoice; for behold, your reward is great in heaven"** (verses 21, 22, &c.)*

Hear what St. James says of riches and tribulations: *"**My brethren, count it all joy when you shall fall into divers temptations; knowing that the trying of your faith worketh patience; and patience hath a perfect work."**** (chap, i.) Here he does not say: Bear, endure, be patient; but, Rejoice, yea, ***"count it all your joy:"*** that is, receive your tribulation, not as an affliction, but as matter for great joy. On the other hand, he thus speaks of riches: ***" Go to, now, ye rich men, weep and howl in your miseries which shall come upon you:"*** and in the preceding chapter he adds: ***" Be afflicted, and mourn, and weep: let your laughter be turned into mourning, and your joy into sorrow."*** (ch. iv. 9.)

But whence is it, that persecution makes a man happy, which ought rather [1] make him miserable? Much could be said on this point: but I will make only one remark, that persecution is like a furnace of burning fire. And as fire prepares our food, clears silver of its dross, and proves gold; so also does persecution, if patiently endured, prepare sinners for receiving grace; it purges the imperfect, and proves the just, and thus all are wonderfully benefited. A sinner is "raw flesh" as it were, which, unless it be properly cooked, is cast away as not fit to be eaten by man.

For a sinner is full of bad humours of the concupiscence of the flesh, which is Luxury: of the concupiscence of the eyes, which is Avarice: and of pride, which is Ambition. But if he pass through the furnace of persecution, he is " cooked" in such a manner, as to be fit to be presented at the table of the Lord. When persecution or tribulation comes, then we forget our passions, our avarice, ambition, &c.; and we begin to be entirely different men. But a just man, though imperfect, and not subject to enormous crimes, may yet be indulgent to his flesh, a lover of pleasure, a lover of gain, and of the vanities of the world. He is therefore like to silver full of much dross.

But if the furnace of persecution should overtake him, and he bear it with patience, then the dross will gradually be separated from the silver; he will begin to be recollected, to meditate on heavenly things, to abstain from carnal desires; in fine, to live justly, soberly, and piously in this world, and to expect that blessed hope, and the coming of the glory of the great God. Lastly, a man perfect in charity is gold; but he has to be proved by the fire of persecution, lest others [2] should suspect, that he was debased gold, not pure gold; for when it is seen that he patiently endures the fire of persecution, not only is he acknowledged by others to be what he appears to be, but he himself also acquires a greater hope, and a more secure expectation of the kingdom of heaven. ***"Tribulation," saith the Apostle, "worketh patience; and patience trial; and trial hope; and hope confoundeth not."*** (Epistle to the Romans, chap. v. 3, &c.) Thus God daily more and more exalts his friend that is proved by tribulation, till at length He brings him to a share of his kingdom and happiness. Behold what is the fruit of patience in affliction! But it is strange to see how few make use of these advantages, although they are open to all.

Affliction is everywhere to be found, everywhere to be met with at home, on a journey, in the forum, in the temple, for in all places the wicked oppress the good. Wherefore, most true are the words of the Apostle: ***"All that will live godly in Christ Jesus, shall suffer persecution."*** But we, delicate soldiers, either fly from this proving furnace, or when we have received an injury we throw it back on our adversary: so that we not only refuse to suffer persecution, but we even cause it. And

those are to be found a man's enemies of his own house-
hold that applaud him who retaliates an injury,[3] and yet
such people who despise the precepts of Christ, wish to
be called Christians!

THE FOURTH MEANS OF ATTAINING THE KINGDOM OF GOD.

BUT because this doctrine is very difficult, and very few understand it, and much less wish to experience it, therefore our Leader hath pointed out the fourth "way," and this very narrow. He says: **"** ***The kingdom of heaven suffereth violence, and the violent alone bear it away"*** (St. Matthew, chap. xi. 12.) As if He had said: I am aware that it will appear a paradox to men, that those should be happy who are poor, and those miserable who are rich; on the contrary, that we should rejoice in afflictions, and weep in prosperity; neither was I ignorant, that few are they who would wish to lose present goods, in order to acquire future ones; and to choose present evils, that so they might avoid those to come. But I who am Truth, must speak the truth; therefore I now add, that the kingdom of heaven can be taken only by the violent; therefore have I said in another place: ***"How hardly shall they that have riches enter into the kingdom of heaven. For it is easier for a camel to pass through the eye of a needle, than for a rich man to enter into the kingdom of heaven."*** And again: ***"How narrow is the***

gate, and strait is the way that leadeth to life, and few there are that find it !"

And in another place I have said, that the kingdom of heaven is like unto a treasure hidden in a field; and to a precious " pearl which cannot be purchased unless we sell everything; hence it is necessary for us to be deprived of every thing on earth, if we wish to possess in heaven this heavenly treasure and precious pearl. In St. Luke I have likewise plainly assured you: ***"Everyone of you that doth not renounce all that he possesseth, cannot be my disciple"*** (chap. xiv. ver. 33.) And although this "renunciation" is to be understood as relating to the affection of the mind; yet since a real disposition to part with all temporal goods, should the honour of God or our own salvation require it, is no easy matter, and which few accomplish.

I have therefore added other similitudes concerning him who wished to build a tower, and had not wherewith to finish it; and of a king who was about to wage war against another king, and had not sufficient forces to engage with him, with any hope of victory. Now if the erection of a tower, without a great sum of money, and a war against a powerful king, without a great army, be difficult and almost impossible things, how much more difficult will it be to accomplish both of these at the same time? But we must accomplish both, if we wish to gain heaven; for a tower is to be built which must reach to heaven; that is, good works are to be performed which will merit eternal life: and at the same time, we have to fight against numerous and powerful enemies, viz. impure spirits, who with all their might endeavour to hinder the building of the tower.

We have a figure of this conflict in the children of Israel, who, when they wished to rebuild Jerusalem that had been destroyed by the Chaldeans, were obliged with incredible toil and anxiety, to build with one hand and to fight with the other, on account of the neighbouring nations that attacked them." ***"Of them that built on the wall and that carried burdens, and that laded; with one of his hands he did the work, and with the other he held a sword."*** (2 Esdras, chap. iv. 17.)

From these considerations it is manifest, that the kingdom of heaven cannot be obtained without great toil and labour, by those who are wedded to earthly objects, who do not tame the concupiscence of the flesh, nor have learned to fight with their invisible enemies. But he who wishes seriously to apply, by the grace of God, to Christian perfection; to consider, not carelessly, but most attentively, the words of Christ; and to follow His example and that of the saints, gradually the way will be opened before him; his strength will increase; his enemies diminish; and by the charity of God in Christ Jesus, his yoke will begin to appear sweet and his burden light; and then will be accomplished the words of Isaias: ***"They that hope in the Lord shall renew their strength, they shall take wings as eagles, they shall run and not be weary, they shall walk and not faint."*** (chap. xl. ver. 31.) And they will exclaim with the royal Prophet: ***" I have run the way of thy commandments, when thou didst enlarge my heart."***

It was not truly a difficult thing for St. Antony to spend so many sleepless nights; nay, even the night appeared too short through the sweetness he enjoyed from the divine contemplation, for he complained of the sun, saying: ***"Why dost thou hinder me by rising at this time, and withdrawing me from the brightness of my true Light?"*** [Cassian, (Colloquy 9th, chap. 31.)] Neither was it difficult for him [1] to prolong their fasting through a whole week, since they were refreshed with the heavenly bread of divine contemplation. Neither was it painful for St. Augustine, to be deprived of those carnal pleasures to which he had been addicted from his youth, when once he began to taste the sweetness of divine love, and the delight of inward contemplation. Wherefore no one, whoever he may be, ought to despond; but rather to hope in the power of the Most High, who, as He hath made us for Himself, will also draw us to Himself and place us in His kingdom, by the merits of His Son, by whose precious blood we have been redeemed.

Wherefore, Christian soul, thou shouldst not despond on account of the difficulty of the way, but hope in the Lord, who would not have invited thee to seek His kingdom in the first place, unless He had been prepared to aid thee by His most powerful assistance. Courageously therefore commence the journey. There is no occasion here for deliberation. If the labour be great, great also is the reward; and if the numerous forces of the enemy hinder thee, greater is the power of God who assists thee. And if many of every age and sex have been enabled to arrive at the kingdom by this way, why mayest not thou also obtain the same?

They were not made of stone or iron, but of flesh; they were mortal and frail, and therefore they could do nothing of themselves, but only by the Lord their God. Canst not thou therefore, though weak and infirm, do the same by the Lord thy God?

"Cast thyself upon Him," says St. Augustine, ***"fear not; He will not withdraw Himself, that thou shouldst fall: securely cast thyself upon Him; He will receive thee, and will help thee."*** (Lib. 8. Confess, cap. 11)

God is faithful, He cannot deceive. Two things only are required of thee; one, that thou most firmly resolve to prefer the glory of God and thy eternal salvation before all things else; the other, that thou confide not in thy own strength, or in thy own wisdom, but in the power of God and His infinite love. If thou wilt comply with these two conditions, "the crooked shall become straight, and the rough ways plain" to thee; and thou wilt serve the Lord with joy and exultation, and "wilt sing in the ways of the Lord; for great is the glory of the Lord"

BOOK II

ON THE BEAUTY OF THE CITY OF GOD.

"**G**LORIOUS *things are said of thee, O city of God:*" wherefore I have desired to behold thy glory, meditating upon it through a glass in an obscure manner. But our first consideration is, why the happiness of the saints, which in the Holy Scripture is called the kingdom of heaven, is also called the *"City of God."* This appears to me to be the reason; because as it is called a kingdom on account of its extent, so also it ought to be called a " City," on account of its beauty. One might suppose, when he heard of a vast and extensive kingdom, that there are in it many deserts, many wild uncultivated places, and mountains fit only for the habitation of beasts, besides inaccessible rocks, forests, and precipices, & c. But since all these are far removed from the happiness of the saints, the Holy Spirit therefore teaches us, that the kingdom of heaven is like to a most "beautiful city; and although it is of a boundless extent, yet the whole is so glorious as to appear a most populous and opulent city. In large cities especially are to be seen beautiful temples, splendid palaces, most delightful gardens, noble forums, fountains, columns, pyramids, obelisks, theatres, towers, and other buildings for the use of the public.

How beautiful would Italy be, if the barren Apennines were removed, and all the country shone like Rome did [1] under Augustus Cæsar! From being of brick, he made it of marble. And how beautiful would Syria have been formerly, if all parts had been like Jerusalem such as it was before its destruction by the Romans! Josephus gives such a description of it, that its magnificence must have been the admiration of the whole world (Vide Lib. vi. de Bello Judaico, cap. 6.) of it the Prophet justly sings, "Glorious things are said of thee, O city of God;" and yet it had not then arrived at that eminence to which Herod the Great carried it, after the reigns of David and Solomon. How beautiful also would Chaldæa, and all Assyria and Mesopotamia, and the whole East have been, had these been enclosed within the walls of Babylon! Pliny and Strabo give such descriptions of its magnitude and beauty, that they seem incredible: hence Babylon was considered one of the seven wonders of the world. Now, what must that city above be the heavenly Jerusalem, which embraceth the whole kingdom of heaven?

This kingdom so far excels all other kingdoms in glory, majesty, and extent, that the whole appears but one city, most beautiful, most noble. Truly, then, this heavenly city is such, that no one can seriously think of it without frequently aspiring after it; and no one can desire it without immediately leaving all things to possess it, and never resting till he find it. Hear how Tobias, exulting in spirit, speaks of this city: ***"Thou shalt shine with a glorious light, and all the ends of the earth shall worship thee The gates of Jerusalem shall be built of sapphire and of emerald, and all the walls thereof round about of precious stones. And all its streets shall be paved with white and clean stones;***

and Alleluia shall be sung in its streets." (chap, xiii. 21, 22.)

And St. John also, in his Apocalypse, agrees with Tobias: *The building of the wall thereof was of jasper-stone; but the city itself pure gold, like to clear glass. And the foundations of the walls of the city were adorned with all manner of precious stones and every several gate was of one several pearl; and the street of the city was pure gold, as it were transparent glass."* (chap, xxi.) But we must not suppose the heavenly Jerusalem to be in reality adorned with gold and precious stones, but by this mode of expression we are to understand, that the heavenly city is as much superior to earth as gold is to dirt, as pearls to common stone, the stars to candles, the sun to a torch, and mortal architects to God, the immortal Creator of all things. But as we intend to speak of the beauty of all the parts of the city of God, we shall dwell no longer on this point.

ON THE CONCORD AND PEACE OF THE CITY OF GOD.

ANOTHER reason why the kingdom of heaven is called the "city of God," appears to be this, because a kingdom usually contains an almost infinite number of people, differing one from another in their language, manners, and laws; where many have never seen each other, and much less formed any acquaintance. But a city includes those only who are of the same language, the same customs, and who are governed by the same laws.

Wherefore, heaven is called both "a kingdom and a city" because, although the inhabitants of this heavenly kingdom are almost innumerable, and as St. John tells us, are collected from "all nations, and tribes, and peoples, and tongues," and also divided into angels, archangels, principalities, powers, dominations, thrones, cherubim, and seraphim, who are much more numerous than men, and are distinguished, not by nations, and peoples, and tongues, but by a specific diversity of nature; yet all these are true citizens, living in concord and unanimity, and governed by one only law of charity.

Wherefore, all have but one heart and one soul.

And because charity is contrary to hatred, envy, contention, discord, strife, and other vices, therefore anger, contention, envy, &c., are far removed from this holy city of Jerusalem: charity alone reigneth, and with it justice, peace, and "joy in the Holy Ghost" In the beginning of creation there was a great battle in heaven between Michael, the archangel, and the dragon; but Michael, and the angels who remained firm with him in faith and obedience to their Lord, gained the victory over the dragon and his angels, who by their pride had fallen away from God." [1]

"And that great dragon was cast out, that old serpent who is called the devil and Satan, who seduceth the whole world; and he was cast unto the earth, and his angels were thrown down with him." (Apoc. chap. xii. 9.) From that time the holy city of Jerusalem *"hath placed peace in its borders;"* nor has the sound of the war- trumpet been heard therein, neither will it be heard there for ever.

What then can be sweeter, what more blessed than this city? They who know the evils of war, its depredations, slaughter, rapine, sacrileges, &c., can easily imagine the sweetness of peace. But, leaving aside war, who has not experienced in his own city, and even in his own house, how disagreeable it is to have anything to do with passionate men, who take the worst view of all our actions? "Depart from the unjust, and evil shall depart from thee," saith Ecclesiasticus. But where shall we go, and not find the unjust? and if they are everywhere to be found, evils will certainly be found also, as long as we remain in this land of exile. Hear how the same Ecclesiasticus speaks of a wicked woman: *"It will be more agreeable to abide with a lion and a dragon than to dwell with a wicked woman."* (chap, xxv.)

Now, if the partner of one s life becomes a lion and a dragon on account of her wickedness, to how many afflictions are men exposed! ***"All that will live godly in Christ Jesus shall suffer persecution,"*** says the apostle. (2 Timothy, chap. iii. 12.) How unhappy, therefore, is the city of this world, wherein we are obliged to bear with so many enemies, and to fight our way. If we wish to be devout, we shall be persecuted by men; and if, to avoid their persecution, we become wicked, we shall then incur the indignation of our supreme and almighty King, who will punish us, and, both alive and dead, will take vengeance, for His anger no one can resist. Oh, unfortunate and miserable country, where no one can escape from war or persecution, where no one can find true peace! ***Let us therefore, with our whole heart, love and praise that heavenly city, from which alone every affliction is banished, and where no war, no hatred, no strife, can ever gain admittance.***

ON THE LIBERTY OF THE CITY OF GOD.

A THIRD reason why the kingdom of God is called a "city," is because a kingdom is in the form of a monarchy, and this seems opposed to liberty. But all the citizens of heaven are free, and Jerusalem, our mother above, is also *"free,"* according to St. Paul in his Epistle to the Galatians. This blessed Apostle knew what he was speaking of, since he had been rapt up into the third heaven, into paradise, and became acquainted with the nature of the city.

Wherefore, as a kingdom implies servitude, and a city liberty, that kingdom alone may be called a city where they who obey the king are free. But the blessed in heaven possess not one simple liberty, but one that is manifold. In the first place, all the inhabitants are free from the servitude of sin, because the first liberty possessed in the earthly paradise was to be able not to sin; but the second enjoyed in heaven is far more excellent *" not to be able to sin,"* as St. Augustine teaches."(De Correptione et Gratiâ, cap. ii.)

Another liberty [1] is being free from the servitude of death. Adam in the earthly paradise was free, so that he could have escaped death: the Sons of Adam in the heavenly paradise are free, so that they cannot die. You must not be surprised at our making liberty to consist in not being able to do anything; because " not being able to sin, and not able to die," indicate the height of liberty from the servitude of sin, and the servitude of mortality. For he who cannot sin, is not only free from sin, but is also so far removed from its servitude that he feels a sure security sin will never prevail within him; and he who cannot die is not only free from death, but he is so far removed from it that he feels confident death will never approach him.

This liberty God alone naturally enjoys, for the Apostle says: ***"Who alone hath immortality."*** And although the angels and souls endowed with reason are said to be naturally immortal, because they have within them no principle of corruption; yet God, who made them, can also destroy them. But, as we have already remarked, the angels and blessed spirits are certain that they will never sin and never die, and therefore they are completely free from the servitude of sin and of death; this is a most honourable participation in the Divine liberty.

The third liberty consists in being free from ***"necessity"*** in general. Now man is obliged to eat, drink, sleep, and labour, at one time to stand or walk, and at another to lie down. But the saints in heaven are not subject to any such necessity, but are free from every necessity, which is the liberty of the glory of the Sons of God, as St. Paul expresses it in his Epistle to the Romans. How great this liberty is, first poor people, then spiritual men, and thirdly the rich of this world bear witness.

What labour the poor endure that they may provide food and clothing for themselves and children! and how greatly would they thank those who would free them from such a state of servitude! Many even rob and plunder others, and suffer themselves to be led into bad habits, to be enabled to support themselves; for they say with the unjust steward in the Gospel, ***"To dig I am unable, to beg I am ashamed; I know what I will do. I will defraud my Master that is; by theft and injustice I will free myself from His servitude."***

But by this mode of acting we fall into a far more grievous servitude, viz., the servitude of sin and the devil, the most bitter enemy of the human race. Holy men, who give themselves up to heavenly contemplation, consider the servitude of attending to the body to be a grievous burden, because it standeth in need of many things, and steals a great part of their time from other more important concerns. Eusebius, in his Ecclesiastical History,(Lib. 2 cap. 16.) ***relates from Philo that the first Christians of Alexandria, living under St. Mark the Evangelist, were so taken up with their heavenly meditations as never to taste any food until after sunset, that thus they might give the whole day and a great part of the night to such spiritual employment: scarcely did they allow any portion for the refreshment of the body.***

The same historian tells us, that some forgot their food for three days together, and others continued their fast for six days. ***Cassian in his Colloquies, and Theodoret in his History, testify that many holy hermits were accustomed to the same thing. Wherefore, to all these the servitude of the body was most grievous, and with the Apostle they exclaimed: " Unhappy man that I am, who shall deliver me from the body of this death?"*** But to the inhabitants of this world, and especially to those who are rich, this servitude does not appear grievous, but were they wise they would think differently .

They are addicted to excessive eating and drinking, and love to sleep on soft couches, and when they exceed the bounds of moderation, they fill their bodies with diseases, and to get free from them they are obliged to take bitter medicine, and to endure many sharp pains. Wherefore they are necessitated, whether willing or unwilling, either to remain enemies to God and to bear His terrible wrath, or to fight against the concupiscence of the flesh by temperance and sobriety. This is doubtless a most laborious and dangerous war; but thus both poor and rich, the good and the wicked, would be free from a most painful "necessity" and miserable servitude.

The fourth liberty consists in being free from obedience to the law and the divine precepts, for " the law is not made for the just man, but for the unjust," as St. Paul mentions in His Epistle to Timothy. None are more just than the blessed, who are confirmed in justice, and cannot therefore become unjust. It is true, indeed, that to the just living in this world, the law is not a threatening one, because of their own accord they willingly obey it; nevertheless, it cannot be denied but that it is a law which directs and binds them to do that which is commanded, and to avoid that which is forbidden. But the just, who enjoy the liberty of the Sons of God, stand in need of no law, because they behold all justice in the divine "Word," and, being confirmed in perfect charity, they cannot but accomplish the will of God. Great, then, is this liberty which frees them from every solicitude, and which is so opposed to captivity and the servitude of those unhappy beings, who, with their hands and feet bound, are "cast into the exterior darkness" and into the "furnace of fire," which they can neither endure nor avoid. And yet either one or the other of these abodes will be the lot of every son of Adam. But, alas! many are so blinded by the smoke of present honours, or by the dust of earthly goods, that they see not these things, neither do they consider them, ***" until sudden destruction"*** come upon them: then their torments open their eyes, which before their sins had shut.

ON THE SITUATION AND FORM OF THE CITY OF GOD.

BUT let us now turn toward the Celestial city, and attentively consider its situation, form, foundation, gates, walls, and streets. It is situated on the holy mountains: thus we read in the Psalmist, "The foundations thereof are in the holy mountains ;" with this St. John agrees in the Apocalypse, where he says: ***"And he took me up in spirit to a great and high mountain: and he showed me the holy city Jerusalem, coming down out of heaven from God."*** (chap. xxi. 10.) The situation of a city on a mountain is very convenient and useful, both for the purity of the air and as a fortification. But what mountains are higher than heaven? and what mountain is exalted above all mountains, except the heaven of heavens, of which David speaks, ***"The heaven of heavens is the Lords!" This is that mountain for which the same Prophet sighed when he said, "Who shall ascend into the mountain of the Lord, or who shall stand in His holy place?" And from this he implored and expected assistance, saying, " I have lifted up my eyes to the mountains, from whence help shall come to me."***

Wherefore, the situation of the city of God is so high as to shut out everything that could in any way disturb its peace and harmony. It is higher than dust, thorns, and briars, or the poisonous bite of animals can reach: it is so high that neither vapours nor clouds, neither hail, nor thunder, fire, nor lightning can terrify it: in fine, it is so high that those impure birds, which St. Paul, in his Epistle to the Ephesians, calls "The spirits of wickedness in the high places," can never reach it.

The form of the City of God is square, for thus St. John tells us: ***"And the city lieth in a foursquare, and the length thereof is as great as the breadth."***(Apoc. XXI:16) This expression signifies nothing more, than that admirable and perfect justice which is to be found in the city, where nothing unjust, nothing contradictory, nothing deformed can gain admittance. Thus St. Augustine explains the Psalm, "Mirabile in æquitate," that is, in justice. And truly wonderful will it be, to behold the innumerable inhabitants of this city, all endowed with perfect free-will; and yet throughout all eternity nothing wrong or imperfect will be found in any one of them, either in thought, word, or deed. Justly, therefore, does this city lie in a square, so that the breadth should not, in the least point, exceed the length, nor the length the breadth. This figure of a square may also signify, that the breadth of its heavenly treasures is equal to their length; because as the abundance of goods will be infinite, so also will their duration.

In the Scripture, breadth is applied to multiplicity, length to the duration of a thing. Thus, in the third Book of Kings, the great wisdom of Solomon is said to be "largeness of heart *(Latitude Cordis)* as the sand that is on the sea- shore:" and in the 90th Psalm, duration of time is called " length of days." There will, therefore, be in the city of our God, as much breadth as length, because there will be an immensity of good things, together with an eternal duration of them. St. John also

adds, that the height of the city is as great as its breadth,
[1] because the goods of the heavenly Jerusalem will not
only be great and eternal, but also most noble and
sublime.

It is of little consequence, that Vitruvius and Veg-
etius do not approve of a square for the situation of a
city: they speak of a city that feareth an enemy. But the
Scripture speaketh of that holy city, which hath placed
peace in its borders, and to which no evil can come on
account of its height.

ON THE FOUNDATIONS
AND GATES OF THE CITY
OF GOD.

THE foundation is of such a nature, that the city alone may justly be called the foundation. Thus speaks St. Paul in his Epistle to the Hebrews, ***"For he looked for a city that hath foundations; whose builder and maker is God"*** (chap. xi. 10.) The Apostle gives the reason, why Abraham did not build a city in the land of promise, but dwelt therein as a stranger: the reason was, because he knew that the land of promise was but a figure of a better land of promise; and, therefore, he was unwilling to build a house or city that would perish, because he looked for a city that had a strong foundation, ***"whose builder and maker is God."***

Wherefore, this heavenly city alone truly and properly hath a foundation, since it was built by God to endure for ever. The cities which Cain, Nimrod, Ninus, Nabuchodonosor, Romulus, &c., founded, have often fallen, and at the last day will entirely be destroyed: this proves that they had no solid foundation. Hence, we may understand how much wiser were the Patriarchs than we are, who, although they lived more than double the number of our years, and were obliged to wait so many thousands of years before they could enter the heavenly city; yet they built neither cities nor houses, but dwelt in tabernacles, as strangers and pilgrims, believing with an assured hope that they were destined to inhabit an Eternal city in heaven, and that all things on earth would quickly perish.

But we, who live to such a short period, and who can, if we wish, immediately after death, enter into that most blessed city, so labour in erecting and adorning buildings on earth, as if we were either never to die, or else had no expectations of entering Heaven. In this point, we certainly imitate not the faithful Patriarchs, but unbelieving Infidels: and yet we are Christians, and we know that Christ and his Apostles built neither a city, nor a tower, nor had even a house; neither did they wish for one.

But still, I do not blame the princes of this world, although Christians, for building new cities: nor private individuals for erecting houses for their own convenience. For we know that David, a pious king, enlarged the city of Jerusalem, and built in it a royal palace, as we read in the Second Book of Kings. We also know that St. Lewis, king of France, erected in Palestine, at his own expense, several cities for the Christians: neither are we ignorant, that it is but just Princes should possess more magnificent habitations than private men, and patricians more than the common people.

But we only require moderation, and condemn extravagance, especially when individuals wish for the palaces of princes; and princes, not content with their palaces, erect immense buildings that look like towns: in fine, we blame a too great affection for temporal goods, as if our chief happiness consisted in them: but we praise a contempt for the world, joined with the humility of Christ.

The gates of this city are said by St. John to be made of precious stones, and the walls of the jaspar stone; but the whole city itself of pure gold. All this signifies that every part is precious, pure, and transparent; for we know that pearls are both precious and white: the jaspar-stone is sometimes found white, and other times green. But St. John says: *"And the light thereof was like to a precious stone, as to the jaspar- stone, even as crystal:" he adds, "as crystal," to show that he is speaking, not of a green jaspar, or any other colour, but of a white and clear one.*

Thus also when he says, that the streets are of pure gold, he adds, *"like to clear glass;"* that is, transparent and white like crystal. Wherefore, whether we consider the whole city, or the gates, the walls, or the streets, all is precious: nothing is mean, unbecoming, fading; but every thing is beautiful, every thing visible, because there nothing can be found to be hidden or concealed: all behold all things: there no suspicions nor stratagems are admitted. This perhaps is the reason why St. John says in the same place, *"And the gates thereof shall not be shut"* because no darkness, no robbers, no enemies are there, on account of which the gates should be closed at night. This verse is not opposed to the words of the Psalmist, where he praises the heavenly Jerusalem: *"Praise the Lord, O Jerusalem, because he hath strengthened the bolts of thy gates."* (Psalm cxlvii.)

Both the Psalmist and the Evangelist mean this only that in the heavenly Jerusalem, no danger is to be apprehended from enemies or robbers. By the gates being always shut, the one signified, that the divine protection would never permit any enemy to enter the beloved city of God: the other meant, by the gates being always open, that the city was so secure from every evil attack, there was no need of keeping the gates shut, nor of employing any guards. But what do the gates, the walls, and streets Signify? The gates always open signify, that by the passion of Christ admittance has been given to all men, of entering the city of God, and of His angels; *" Christ having overcome the sting of death, hath opened to believers the kingdom of heaven."* And not one only, but twelve gates are there, by which Christians can enter the city: thus St. John tells us*: "On the east, three gates; and on the north, three gates; and on the south, three gates; and on the west, three gates. Therein enter, not the Jews alone, as they imagine; but all nations from every quarter of the earth: nay, so few Jews enter, as to bear no comparison with the others.*

Thus our Lord predicted when He spoke of the centurion: *"Amen I say unto you, I have not found so great faith in Israel. And I say to you, that many shall come from the east and the west, and shall sit down with Abraham, and Isaac, and Jacob in the kingdom of heaven: but the children of the kingdom shall be cast out into the exterior darkness."* *'amen dico vobis non inveni tantam fidem in Israhel. Dico autem vobis quod multi ab oriente et occidente venient et recumbent cum Abraham et Isaac et Iacob in regno caelorum'* (Matt. viii: 10,11).

And in the parable of the vineyard, *"Therefore I say to you, that the kingdom of God shall be taken from you, and shall be given to a nation yielding the fruits thereof."* But this is most clearly expressed in St. Luke: *"There shall be weeping and gnashing of teeth, when you shall see Abraham, and Isaac, and Jacob, and all the prophets in the kingdom of God, and yourselves thrust out. And there shall come from the east and the west, and the north and the south, and shall sit down in the kingdom of God."* (Luke xiii 28,29)

Three gates are said to be from every part of the world, making in all twelve, because an entrance will be open, not only from the east and the west, the north and the south, but from the beginning of the east, from the middle, and from the end of the east, and so of the other parts. Another explanation may perhaps please us more,

that the three gates are fixed to each part of the heavenly city, to express the mystery of the Trinity and the
three most necessary virtues: for all those enter from the
four quarters of the globe, who being baptized in the
name of the three divine Persons, have persevered to the
end in Faith, Hope, and Charity.

ON THE WALLS AND STREETS OF THE CITY OF GOD.

THE walls of the city signify nothing more, than the divine protection, which alone is sufficient to guard the city, without the aid of soldiers, arms, or towers. ***"And I will be, saith the Lord, a wall of fire round about: and I will be in glory in the midst thereof."*** *"Et ego ero ei ait Dominus murus ignis in circuitu et in gloria ero in medio eius"* (Zacharias ii.5) Truly admirable promise! "I will be a wall of fire round about" to restrain the enemy: " and I will be in glory in the midst thereof" to honour the citizens.

As if He had said: Fire burns and shines: I will therefore burn mine enemies, and enlighten my friends: thus will I be a "fire round about," and a light of glory in the midst thereof. This St. John explains where he says: "And the city hath no need of the sun, nor of the moon to shine in it. For the glory of God hath enlightened it, and the Lamb is the lamp thereof." (Apoc xxi 23) The brightness of God, as a sun, illumines their souls; and Christ, the Lamb of God, illumines the body. But Christ is said to be a "lamp," not because it is necessary in the night, but with reference to his divinity: for if the just shall shine like the sun in the kingdom of God, as our Lord tells us in St, Matthew; how much more glorious will Christ appear not as a lamp, but as the chief Sun enlightening the city of God!

And, therefore, St. John adds, *"For there shall be no night." (*Apoc xxi 25) *The streets of the city comprehend the whole space which is within the circumference of the walls. This is the habitation of the heavenly citizens - all of which is pure gold; that is, an ardent and pure charity which embraceth all, and by which all live in each through mutual love: and not only all in all, but all dwell in God, and God in all: " for he that abideth in charity, abideth in God, and God in him. "* (1 St. John iv. 16.)

And that this might be accomplished, Christ our Lord asked of His Father in that prayer which he made before His passion, in presence of all His apostles, saying: *"And not for them only do I pray, but for them also who through their word shall believe in me: That they may all be one, as thou Father in Me, and I in Thee; that they also may be one in Us."* (St. John xvii.20, 21.) O blessed city which, placed on the highest mountain, enjoyest the purest air! Thou art founded on a rock, that thou mayest have eternal strength: thy gates shine as pearls, and are always open to those that enter: God is thy wall, that continually surrounds thee by His protection, and adorns thee as a precious jasper stone: thy street is charity, purer than any gold, clearer than any crystal, which maketh all that dwell within thee, to be of one heart and one soul; which filleth them with ineffable joy, and crowneth them with eternal peace: *"My soul longeth and fainteth"* for thy courts. *"*

What can be sweeter to one labouring and groaning amidst a corrupt nation -amongst false brethren in a world *" seated in iniquity,"* than to flee away to a kingdom wherein the sweetest peace is found, wherein charity alone reigneth? *"When shall I come and ap-*

pear before the face of my God?" (Psalm xli.) What more desirable for a soul that loves God, than to behold her Beloved to be seen by her Beloved and by an intimate and most joyful union, to dwell within Him, and He in her! It may indeed appear an intolerable boldness, that dust and ashes should sigh after thy courts, O holy city, and a still greater audacity, that a vile creature should aspire to the embraces of his Creator. But He will excuse this boldness, since He hath given it unto us, when he asked the Father, that "all might be one;" and that as the Father is in the Son, and the Son in the Father, so also we might be one in both.

ON THE TEMPLE OF THE CITY OF GOD.

BUT there is something else wanting in the city, viz: a temple to praise God, and to take our meat and drink: of garments we shall stand in no need. For if in the earthly paradise Adam and Eve required none, much less will the Saints want them in their heavenly paradise, where all are clothed with light as with a garment. And not only Adam and Eve required food, but also the angels themselves, as Raphael saith: ***"But I use an invisible meat and drink, which cannot be seen by men.***" (Tobias xii. 19.) And so also in relation to this temple, St. John thus speaks in his Apocalypse: ***"And I saw no temple therein. For the Lord God Almighty are the temple thereof, and the Lamb."*** (chap, xxi.)

That St. John saw no temple in the holy city, must not appear strange to us: in the church militant temples are erected, for four reasons: That the word of God might be preached to the people; that the sacraments and sacrifices might be celebrated; that public prayer might be offered to God, and Psalms sung to the Lord with joy and gladness. Now the preaching of God s word will cease in heaven, where the uncreated Word itself will clearly speak unto all, according to the prediction of Jeremiah the prophet: ***"And they shall teach no more every man his neighbour, and every man his brother, saying: "Know the Lord: for all shall know me from the least of them even to the greatest, saith the Lord." (chap. xxi. 34.)***

Sacraments and sacrifice likewise will not be necessary there, where neither sin is to expiated, nor signs are required, because the thing signified will then be made manifest. Prayer and praise are here on earth given to God in sacred temples dedicated unto Him, because He hath promised to have His eyes and ears open to the prayers of those who should gather together in His name; thus He spoke to Solomon in the 2nd Book of Paralipomenon: ***"My eyes also shall be open, and my ears attentive to the prayer of him who shall pray in this place." (chap. vii. 15.) But since in the heavenly city, God will be seen and heard by all, there is no necessity for a temple in that place. Thus we can easily understand what St. John saith: " And I saw no temple therein:" but why has he added, " For the Lord God Almighty is the temple thereof, and the Lamb?" If no temple be required, why is God himself said to be the Temple of that city, and not only God, but the " Lamb " also? Or who shall explain for us, how God and the Lamb are called " Temples " in heaven? And what use hath this temple in heaven?***

In the holy Scripture it is usual for one sentence to serve as an explanation of another, or an obscure passage to be made intelligible by another that is clearer. In the 90th Psalm it is said: ***"He who dwelleth in the aid of the Most High, shall abide under the protection of the God of heaven."*** The meaning of these words is: he who is united to God by a sure confidence, abides as it were in God, in whom he dwells securely, and is protected from all evil. The same may be said of prayer and praise; for he that by an intimate reverence is joined to God, makes, as it were, a house for himself in God, that so whilst living in it, he may praise God and pray unto Him as he ought.

Thus, therefore, the Lord God Almighty is the "Temple" in heaven of the holy city, since these blessed citizens, most attentively considering the omnipotence of God, and thus united to Him by an intimate reverence, dwell in Him, and offer Him worthy praise. So also when they consider the merits of Christ, who as an innocent Lamb delivered himself an oblation, and a victim to God as an odour of sweetness, they are intimately united with Him by love: and reposing in Him as in a temple, they pray for us, and doubtless find the eyes and ears of God open, so that whatsoever they ask they obtain for us.

But if, to praise God and to intercede for us, these blessed citizens dwell in Him and in Christ, as in a temple, what must we do who neither see God nor Christ?! would that by the grace of God, we could so praise Him and pray unto Him, that being first united to Him by true humility, and a deep reverence from the consideration of His Supreme Majesty, we could dwell in Him as in a most sacred temple! Then not carelessly or with distraction, but most attentively and devoutly should we sing our grateful praises to God, and offer up to the Lord prayers that would benefit ourselves and our brethren; then would these words be fulfilled: *" **The sacrifice of praise shall glorify me: and there is the way by which will show him the salvation of God.** "* (Psalm xlix.)

The divine praises, offered up on the altar of the heart by the fire of charity, ascend as an odour of wonderful sweetness; and they obtain for us, that our path may be opened and our heart enlightened, to behold the salvation which God hath prepared for those that love

Him. But all these benefits those miserable men lose, who pray and sing the divine praises with distraction, and a voluntary dryness of heart; they participate with others in the labour of singing and praying, but they enjoy not the divine consolation, nor a foretaste of heavenly happiness.

ON THE MEAT AND DRINK IN THE CITY OF GOD.

CONCERNING the meat and drink of the city of God, we find these words in the Apocalypse: " ***And he showed me a river of the water of life clear as crystal, proceeding from the throne of God and of the Lamb. And in the midst of the street thereof, and on both sides of the river was the tree of life, bearing twelve fruits, yielding its fruits every month; and the leaves of the tree were for the healing of the nations"*** (chap, xxii.)

I am afraid, that some, judging from these words, may wonder at the scantiness of food in heaven, and. think that more substantial meat is to be found in this land of our exile; since in the Apocalypse we read of nothing, but the fruit of one tree for food, and the water of a river for drink. But those who suppose such a thing should remember, that in the terrestrial paradise, where doubtless there was better food than we have now, Adam was only allowed to eat fruit and herbs, and drink water; but this fruit and water were far superior to all the food and wine of this life, though not so in any degree, to the *"tree of life"* and the living water of the heavenly paradise.

In this vale of misery, all men are sickly and have their sense of taste corrupted by a kind of bitterness, and therefore to remove this nausea, they have invented various kinds of food; but this variety so lessens the nausea, as to increase the disease. In the terrestrial paradise however, men were healthy, for the sweetness and wholesomeness of the food and of the water were such, as to be able perfectly to nourish them, and to their great delight, to keep them in continual health; we may add also, that their food was abundantly supplied, without the labour and toil of procuring it. But the living water and *"the tree of life"* in the city of God, are not like the meat and drink of man in common with animals, such as we have in this world; but so excellent, so great, so divine are they, that the Prophet sings, ***"They shall be inebriated with the plenty of thy house, and thou shalt make them drink of the torrent of thy pleasure."*** (Psalm xxxv.)

Neither is this meat or drink any thing corporal, but it is spiritual and divine, of which we read in Ecclesiasticus: ***"She will give him the water of wholesome wisdom to drink ;"*** *and the tree of life is that bread, of which it is written in the same place, " with the bread of life and understanding she shall feed him."* (chap. 15.) And as St. Augustine teacheth, ***"in corporal things food is one thing, and drink another," but in spiritual matters, food and drink are the same; that is, wisdom, or understanding, or intelligence, which signify the same thing, is food that nourishes and drink that extinguishes thirst. But by the " living water," wisdom also may be signified, and by the " tree of life," charity; thus St. John in his first Epistle, " We know that we have passed from death to life, because we love the brethren. He that loveth not, abideth in death."*** (chap, iii.14)

To love as well as to understand, are both spiritual actions; wherefore, the drink of the saints in the city of God, is to drink of the living river that springs from the fountain of life, which is God; this means, to enjoy a participation of that wisdom by which God is wise, and which is most profound, high, and unspeakable. The food of the same saints is to eat of the *" tree of life ;"* that is, to enjoy a share of that ineffable love, whereby goodness itself being clearly seen can be loved, and by which God loves Himself, who is infinitely good, and the fountain of all goodness.

What these signify, we cannot, nor shall we be able to understand, until we arrive at this blessed city. But when St. John says, ***"that on both sides of the river is the tree of life, yielding its fruit every month,"*** we must understand the passage metaphorically, that by a comparison taken from corporal things we may understand the spiritual. The blessed Evangelist intended to point out to us the tree of infinite goodness; and that he might do this, he described the tree which grew at the bank of the river, and which from its excellence, being continually watered, produced fruit every month, not every year as others do.

Neither does he wish to intimate, that there is only one tree, but many of the same kind, which are so planted on both sides of the river flowing through the middle of the city, that there is little space between the one and the other; and in this manner, the view of the whole city can be enjoyed, and the flow of the water as well as the fruit of the tree. The goodness of the tree is signified by the words tree of life; its fruitfulness by the production of new fruit every month. Hence it is, that the inhabitants of the city always have fresh and ripe fruit fresh, from having it every month ripe, from having had it the month immediately preceding: it is never rotten, never dry, never insipid. All this signifies, that the food of the blessed, [1] is the best, and never faileth.

That which the holy Evangelist adds concerning the leaves of the tree, "for the healing of the nations" seems to mean, that in this our exile, the fruit of the tree of life itself will never be given unto us, but only its leaves; these, however, although they confer not eternal life, are yet useful in " healing" our disorders, the concupiscence of the flesh, the concupiscence of the eyes, the pride of life, &c., by which all men are enfeebled more or less. These leaves are the divine revelations of the prophets and apostles, sent to us from heaven.! how sweet an odour would these leaves scatter, if we had the spirit of the Lord. Read the Prophets, the Psalmist, the Gospels, the Epistles of SS. Peter, Paul, John, James, Jude, all these breathe humility, charity, and continency, of which the philosophers make no mention."[2]

Wherefore, Christian soul, diligently peruse these leaves, make unto thee from them a daily medicine; and imagine what must be the fruit thereof. And, then despising the husks of swine, ardently sigh for the fruit of Eternal life which is above; think of it, and as long as it is deferred, let the memory of it never depart from thee.

ON THE MYSTICAL FOUNDATION OF THE CITY OF GOD.

WE have already considered one part of the heavenly Jerusalem, let us now consider another part of the structure. A city not only includes foundations, gates, walls, streets, but also a body of citizens, who according to the variety of their functions, are called the foundations, gates or walls. Hence perhaps a city may more properly be named a collection of citizens under the same laws, rather than a collection of houses within the same walls.

Thus Cicero speaks in the Dream of Scipio: " An assembly of men united by laws are called citizens." Now concerning the heavenly city, which consists of citizens, not only St. John mentions it, but also St. Peter in his first Epistle, and St. Paul in his Epistle to the Ephesians.

We have read in the Apocalypse, that in the twelve gates were twelve angels, and thereon were in scribed the names of the twelve tribes of the children of Israel, and in the twelve foundations the twelve names of the twelve apostles of the Lamb. In the first Epistle of St. Peter we read, ***" Unto whom coming as to a living stone, rejected indeed by men, but chosen and made*** *honourable by God; be you also as living stones built up." (chap, ii.) And in St. Paul's Epistle to the Ephesians, " Now therefore you are no more strangers and foreigners, but you are fellow-citizens with the saints, and domestics of God, built upon the foundation of the apostles and prophets, Jesus Christ himself being the chief corner-stone." (chap. ii. ver. 19.)*

In the first place, therefore, the city of God has for its foundations the apostles and prophets, because their doctrine supports the whole fabric. Faith is the beginning of salvation, but faith has been revealed by the prophets and apostles, either by writing or preaching the mysteries of the blessed Trinity, the incarnation, the resurrection of the dead, everlasting glory, eternal torments; others also, which are above human reason, we have learned from the apostles and prophets, to whom God had revealed them.

But although faith has no place amongst the blessed, since what they believed they see, and what is seen is not believed, but known and understood; yet the apostles and prophets are called the ***"Foundations"*** of the heavenly city, because faith being the beginning of salvation, is consequently the beginning of beatitude.

But since St. Peter saith, that we as living stones are built upon Christ, and St. Paul in his first Epistle to the Corinthians, ***"For other foundation no man can lay, but that which is laid, which is Christ Jesus;"*** therefore there is but one foundation, because in the twelve foundations of the apostles Christ existed, as St. Augustine teacheth in his explanation of the 86th Psalm. He himself or His Spirit spoke by them and taught them: hear the apostle Paul, ***"Do you seek a proof of Christ that speaketh in me :" hear Christ himself, " He that heareth you, heareth me;" and again, "It is not you that speak, but the Spirit of your Father that speaketh in you."***

It is certain that the Spirit of the Father and the Son

is one and the same; hence we may conclude, that not only the twelve Apostles are to be included in **" the twelve foundations,"** but all those likewise who first preached the same faith; otherwise St. Paul himself and St. Barnabas, and the seventy disciples who were not in the number of the Apostles, could not be called foundations, nor even the Prophets themselves; and we should make the apostle a liar, [1] who hath said, "that we are built on? the foundation of the apostles and prophets."

But here occurs a rather difficult question; how can Christ be truly the foundation of the building, when he is called by the apostle **" the chief corner-stone;"** and David says of Him, that He is exalted to be the **"head of the corner?"** How can the same stone be in the foundation and at the top? But if we remember that these expressions are metaphorical, we shall easily understand, that to one person contrary names may be applied, on account of the diversity of his functions.

Now not only Christ, who is both God and man, but every prelate is the foundation and the head of his Church, because as " the foundation he ought to bear the weight of the building, the infirmities of all, and therefore he ought to be below all; and yet as " head" of the building, he is appointed to rule all, command all, and be supported by all. Much more justly, therefore, can Christ our Lord be called the foundation of the Church, because He supports us all, and rules us by His power and authority; at the same time, He is placed as the **"Head,"** to connect the two points, and of the Jews and Gentiles to form one people, to rule and govern all.

ON THE MYSTICAL GATE OF THE CITY OF GOD.

LET us now in order consider the gates of the heavenly Jerusalem. According to the general exposition of interpreters, the twelve Apostles are to be understood by the gates: in this explanation they follow St. Augustine in his exposition of the 86th Psalm. But when St. John in the Apocalypse speaks of the **"gates"** he mentions twelve angels and the twelve tribes of the children of Israel, whose names are written on the twelve gates of the city of God: but in that verse he makes no mention of the apostles.

But the opinion of St. Augustine and of those who follow him is not therefore erroneous", for St. John speaks mystically, not literally as a prophet, not as an historian. The whole description is full of mystical significations.[1]

The land of promise, according to all interpreters, was a figure of the heavenly Jerusalem. Abraham was the first to whom the promise was made: **" All the land which thou seest, I will give to thee, and to thy seed for ever." (Genesis xiii. 15.) And St. Paul, in his**

Epistle to the Galatians: To Abraham were the promises made, and to his seed;" and a little lower he adds: "But God gave it to Abraham by promise." Isaac alone was the heir of Abraham, Ismael being excluded, who was the son of the free woman. Thus the Scripture, "For the son of the bond-woman shall not be heir with my son Isaac." Jacob alone was the heir of Isaac, Esau, his brother, being excluded, who sold his birthright.

Hence the prophet Malachias says, *" I have loved Jacob, but have hated Esau ;"* and these words the apostle repeats in his Epistle to the Romans. The heirs of Jacob were all his sons, twelve in number, not one of whom was excluded; and thus the land of promise was divided amongst the twelve tribes of Israel, as we learn from the Book of Josue. This is, therefore, the reason why St. John said in the Apocalypse, that on the twelve gates were inscribed the names of the twelve tribes of the children of Israel; because the entrance into the promised land was a right of inheritance, which belonged to all the children of Israel alone.

But, as we mentioned above,, St. John speaks figuratively, so that by the twelve tribes of Israel are meant the true Israelites, not according to the flesh, but according to faith and the spirit; and therefore the twelve Apostles are included, as well as their spiritual children. For, as St. Paul clearly teaches us in his Epistle to the Romans: *"All are not Israelites that are of Israel, neither are all they that are of the seed of Abraham, children"* *(chap. ix. 6.).* The same Apostle compares Israel to a tree, whose many branches are broken on account of unbelief, and others ingrafted by reason of faith.

Thus, when the Gentiles were converted, they began to be children of Israel, and many of the Jews ceased to be true Israelites. St. Augustine thus proves this point at length (*Epistola ad Asellicum.*) *"Is not this a wonderful and deep mystery, that many, not born of Israel, should belong to Israel, and many not children, though they were of the seed of Abraham? How are they not? How are they sons? It is, that they are not sons of promise, belonging to the grace of Christ, but sons of the flesh, bearing an empty name; and thus, neither are they of Israel as we are, nor are we of Israel like they are: for we are according to a spiritual regeneration, they according to a carnal one In the grand- children of Abraham, the sons of Isaac viz., Jacob and Esau this great and profound mystery appears, of which the Apostle speaks when he had mentioned the sons promised to Abraham as belonging to the grace of Christ.*

This the apostolic and catholic doctrine clearly teaches, that the Jews belong to Sara, according to the flesh, but the Ismaelites to Agar; and, according to the spirit, Christians belong to Sara, Jews to Agar; to Esau likewise, according to the flesh, who is also called Edom, the nation of the Idumeans; to Jacob, who is also called Israel, the nation of the Jews; but, according to the mystery of the Spirit, the Jews to Esau belong, to Israel the Christians."

Thus St. Augustine clearly proves, that Christians are true Israelites, not according to the flesh, but according to the Spirit; and that thereby they are heirs of the land of promise, which is in heaven. Wherefore, the gates of the heavenly Jerusalem have inscribed on them the names of the twelve tribes of Israel, because the gate by which we enter the land of promise is the inheritance of the Sons of God, who alone are true and sincere Christians', the children of the blessed Apostles. These are signified by the true Israelites, that is, the sons of the patriarch Jacob; and when St. John adds, that on the gates were twelve angels, he means that angels are the guardians of those gates, whose office is to prevent any one entering, that has not the right of inheritance.

For this reason, perhaps, St. Michael, the archangel,

is represented with scales in his hands, because by the angels under him he examines the merits of those who aspire to this heavenly city.

ON THE MYSTICAL STONES OF THE CITY OF GOD.

T HE rest of the building consists of stones; and these are all the faithful, who are built up," according to the expression of St. Peter and St. Paul in their Epistles; and since this part of the building regards every one, it will be very desirable for us to remember the conditions or qualities which those must possess who desire to be built on the foundation of Christ and the apostles, under the chief corner- stone, Christ Jesus; that so they may not only be in the heavenly city, but may also themselves become the highest and most happy city of God.

Three conditions are requisite to be built on so noble a foundation: 1st. That we be stones; 2nd. That we be living ones; 3rd. That we be well polished, and be cut square. We must therefore be stones, not wood, or hay, or stubble, that we may make the wall solid that is, we should be sober and firm, persevering in faith, in charity, in humility, and obedience to the Commandments, and not allow ourselves to be carried about " by every wind of doctrine," as heretics do; neither should we be carried away by various inordinate desires, as bad Catholics are very often.

These are not used as stones by the builders of the eternal city, for they serve only for cottages which are easily destroyed. In the second place, we should be *"living stones,"* as St. Peter admonishes us, that is, full of charity and spiritual life, such as Christ is, " the corner stone," who, although He died once according to the flesh, yet He always lived according to the Spirit, and after death rose again to die no more. Dead stones build dead edifices, that is, corporal; but a spiritual house, or rather the city of our great King, which is spiritual and celestial, requires spiritual stones, and therefore "living" ones.

Thirdly, we must be square and polished stones, not unpolished or shapeless, because thus it becometh the building of a city that is superior to all others. So Arphaxat the king built the city of Ecbatana of square and polished stones, as we read in the book of Judith; and if King Solomon erected a temple to the Lord so beautifully adorned, what ought to be the building of that Eternal city, which so far exceeds all other cities? But this beautifying of our building must be done on earth, not in heaven; and of this the temple of Solomon was a figure. Thus we read in the third book of Kings: *"And the house when it was in building was built of stones hewed and made ready, so that there was neither hammer nor axe, nor any tool of iron heard in the house when it was building." (chap. vii. 7.)* The reason was, because the stones were cut and prepared at a distance from the house of the Lord; and thus they were so perfectly polished, that, when they were brought to the temple, they were laid in their proper places without the sound of the hammer being heard. In the heavenly Jerusalem, also, the sound of the hammer will not be heard, because there no persecution will be, no tribulation no penitential labour, no sighing, no sorrow, no sadness.

Wherefore, those stones that are chosen for the glory of the heavenly mansions, ought in this vale of tears to be well cut and polished: thus the Church sings:

**"Tunsionibus, pressuris, Expoliti
    Lapides, Suis coaptantur locis,
Per manus Artificis,
Disponuntur permansuri,
Sacris ædificiis."**

Here penitential labour is necessary for us, because ***"we all offend in many things"*** as St. James affirmeth: here our carnal concupiscence must be tamed, our self-will conquered, our body chastised and brought into subjection: here with indefatigable diligence must we oppose the ***" shield of faith"*** against the fiery darts of impure spirits. Therefore, if we cannot bear the stroke of the hammer, how can we, being unpolished, be admitted by the heavenly Architect to form part of the building?!

O! if men could but comprehend how much good they deprive themselves of by flying from this hammer, and being unwilling to endure anything that is difficult, bitter, and contrary to their inclination, assuredly they would then alter their mind, and fast often instead of having their banquets; throwing aside their soft garments, they would put on sackcloth, and give themselves up to watching and prayer, instead of indulging in vain talk; and if they received any injury from false brethren, or from open enemies, they would not think of revenge, but would give thanks to God, and earnestly pray to Him for their calumniators and persecutors: this they would do, because ***" The sufferings of this time are not worthy to be compared with the glory to come, that shall be revealed in*** *us;" and again, That which is at present momentary and light of our tribulation, worketh for us above measure exceedingly an eternal weight of glory."*

And truly, if we consider the "living stones" that have preceded us in the heavenly building, we shall see that all were polished by many strokes of the hammer. Christ Himself, " the corner-stone," and most precious, who stood in need of no polishing, yet suffered for us that He might leave us an example: " Who, when He was reviled, did not revile; when He suffered, He threatened not." All the Apostles could say with St. Paul: " Even unto this hour we both hunger and thirst, and are naked and are buffeted, and have no fixed abode: and we labour, working with our hands: we are reviled, and we bless; we are persecuted, and we suffer it. We are blasphemed, and we entreat; we are made as the refuse of this world, the offscouring of all even until now." (I Epistle to the Corinthians, chap, iv .)

What shall I say of the martyrs? Did not all ascend unto the city of the heavenly Jerusalem, after they had been "cut and polished" by many tribulations and most cruel deaths? I omit mentioning the holy confessors, anchorets, virgins, widows, and all others who served God. Unless these had crucified their flesh, with its vices and concupiscences, and had waged war against themselves, they would not have been admitted to the heavenly building.

But this polishing of *" living stones"* was necessary, not only after the coming of our Saviour, but before also, and from the beginning of the world itself. The first living stone was Abel, cruelly slain by his brother Cain; afterwards came the holy patriarch Joseph, sold by his brothers. The angel Raphael said to Tobias also: Because thou wast pleasing to God, it was necessary that temptation should try thee." He did not say, because thou wast a sinner, and hateful to God, it was necessary that you should be punished with blindness and poverty; but he said, because thou wast pleasing unto God, being just and holy, therefore, as a living stone destined for the heavenly building, it was necessary that you should bear the stroke of the hammer. Who amongst the prophets did not suffer persecution from the impious? What torments did not the holy Machabees endure? Let us hear the apostle Paul speaking of the saints in the old Law, in his Epistle to the Hebrews: ***And others had trials of mockeries and stripes, moreover, also, of bonds and prisons. They were stoned, they were cut asunder, they were tempted, they were put to death by the sword, they wandered about in sheep- skins, in goat skins, in mountains, and in the dens and caves of the earth.*** "(chap. xi. 37, 38.)

What wilt thou say, Christian soul, to these words? If the hammer of the builder did not spare those of whom the world was not worthy, on account of their great sanctity, that so they might be fitly polished for the celestial building, what will become of thee, and of those like thee, who indulge in sin, and consider penitential labours too heavy?

One of these two things is necessary: either that thou suffer in this life or in purgatory, or be deprived of a place in that Edifice above, and made to bear for ever the hammer of hell. Why, therefore, dost thou not choose[1] rather to endure the short and momentary tribulations of this life, than to be condemned to future ones, eternal and intolerable?

Despise not the purgatorial punishments of the world to come; although they are not eternal, yet are they more grievous, and often of longer duration, than any torment of this life. Hear St. Augustine's Explanation of the 37th Psalm***: " It is said, thou shalt be saved, yet so as by fire; and because it is said, "Thou shalt be saved" this fire is contemned; yet it will be more grievous than any torment a man can endure*** *in this life"* He also adds, ***"that the torments will be more severe than the punishments of robbers and the torments of the martyrs :"wherefore, those are mad who despise the fire of purgatory, and dread the tribulations of this present life"***[2] And because in the mouth of two or three witnesses every word shall stand, hear St. Gregory on the third penitential Psalm: ***"I consider this transitory fire to be more intolerable than all present tribulations ;"*** hear St. Bernard in his Sermon on the death of Humbert, a monk: ***"But this know, that, after this life, in purgatory will be required a hundred-fold what hath here been neglected, even unto the last farthing"*** Hear, in fine, ***St. Anselm, in his Explanation of the third chapter of St. Paul's First Epistle to the Corinthians: We must know that this fire is more grievous than anything a man can endure in this life; all the torments of the world are mild in comparison with it, and yet men to avoid them will do whatever they are commanded by others. How much better would it be to do what God commands, that so we might not suffer more grievous torments !"***

ON FLYING FROM THE CITY
OF THIS WORLD.

HAVING spoken of the city of God, it only remains that we now explain in a few words what is especially required, as the condition of our being enrolled citizens of this most blessed kingdom. This can be mentioned in one word; that we renounce the world, and live in it as strangers and pilgrims. We cannot be citizens of the world and of heaven at the same time; and there is no one who flies from the world, who is not immediately received into the midst of the city of God. But let us consider the whole subject more at length.

Two cities are mentioned in the Holy Scripture; the city of this world which commenced in Cain, for he was the first who founded one, as we read in the book of Genesis; and the city of heaven which began in Abel, the founder of which was not Abel, but God, as St. Paul mentions. Babylon was a figure of the first, which signifies "confusion;" but of the latter, Jerusalem was typical, the City of our great king, which means the "vision of peace."

Those are inhabitants of the earthly city who dwell

therein, not only in body, but also in heart, who love the earth, pant after its pleasures, struggle for them, contend for them. Of this city the devil is prince, who having been cast down from heaven, possessed the government of the earth. For although our Lord said when his Passion drew nigh, " now is the judgment of the world, now shall the prince of this world be cast out ;" and although He truly cast him out by His cross, and triumphed over him, according to St. Paul in his Epistle to the Colossians, " And despoiling the principalities and powers, he hath exposed them confidently in open show, triumphing over them in himself;" yet we must not suppose that the devil was entirely "cast out" of the world, or that he has completely lost the dominion of the world, but only that he was cast out of all those, and has lost dominion over them who united themselves with Christ and his heavenly city, and fled from this earthly one.

But that the devil hath yet power over the city of this world, the Apostle teaches us in his Epistle to the Ephesians: ***"For our wrestling is not against flesh and blood, but against principalities and powers, against the rulers of the world of this darkness, against the spirits of wickedness in the high places."*** (chap. vi. 12.)

Wherefore Satan, together with his satellites, yet has power in the world, and is the "ruler" thereof; that is, of earthly- minded men, inhabitants of this earthly city, of which St. John says, ***"It is seated in wickedness."*** As if he had said, the world is united with its chief, who is wicked, or the world is under the power and dominion of a ***"wicked"*** demon. But the inhabitants of the heavenly city, are those who reign happily in its kingdom, and those also, who although they dwell on earth in their mortal body, are far from it in their heart, for their conversation is in heaven, and ***"they desire to be dissolved and to be with Christ."***

But because whilst on earth they are mixed up with its citizens, therefore the Holy Scripture saith, that they are in the world, but not of the world, and in the world, not as citizens, but as strangers and pilgrims; thus St. Peter teacheth, *"Dearly beloved, I beseech you as strangers and pilgrims to refrain yourselves from carnal desires which war against the soul;"* (1 Peter ii.11) on the contrary, the citizens of the world are said in Holy Scripture to be, *"Strangers to the Testament, having no hope of the promise, and without God in this world."*

These words St. Paul makes use of in his Epistle to the Ephesians. Since, then, this is the truth, let no one deceive himself, let no one imagine that he can be a citizen of the world and a citizen of heaven at the same time. Citizens of the world are of the world, citizens of heaven are not of the world. To be of the world, and not to be of the world, are contradictory terms, therefore they cannot be united. Hence those whom earthly objects delight, can have no place in the heavenly city, unless they first flee from the world, unless they renounce it, unless they despise its pleasures.

And since these considerations are important and understood by few, or not considered as they ought to be, therefore that no one may plead ignorance at the Last day, the apostles and evangelists inculcate and repeat them over and over again; hear our Lord: *"You are of this world, I am not of this world ;"* and to the *Apostles He says, "If you had been of the world, the world would love its own: but because you are not of the world, bat I have chosen you out of the world, therefore the world hateth you ;"* hear St. Paul: *"The wisdom of this world is foolishness with God;"* and again, *"You must needs go out of this world that we be not condemned with it."*

Hear St. James: *"Know you not that the friendship of this world is the enemy of God?"* Whosoever, *therefore, will be a friend of this world, becometh an enemy of God;"* (James iv.4) and St. Peter saith: *" Fly the corruption of that concupiscence which is in the world:"* (2 Peter i.4) and St. John; *"Love not the world, nor the things which are in the world. If any man love the world, the charity of the Father is not in him. "* (1 John ii.15)

Hear, in fine, our Lord himself, in his prayer to his Father: *"I pray for them, not for the world do I pray; but for them whom thou hast given me............ And the world hath hated them, because they are not of the world, as I also am not of the world."* (John xvii.9,14)

Here we can most clearly perceive, that the world is thus condemned and excommunicated by God, that Christ does not pray for it all. But if Christ does not pray for the world, how can He say in another place, *" God so loved the world as to give his own beloved Son?"* Doth the Father love the world, and the Son hate it? Or how doth the Son exclude the world from His prayer, whom the Father doth not exclude from His love? St. Augustine, explaining this question, says, that the world for which Christ did not pray, signifies only the wicked, as St. Paul mentions in his first Epistle to the Corinthians; *" That we be not condemned with this world."* It may also be said that Christ did not pray for the world, because what He then was asking for the Apostles, did not in the least regard the world; for He prayed for the gift of perseverance: *" Keep them in thy name."*

And at the same time He prayed that they might possess eternal glory, when He said, *"Father, I will that where I am, they also whom thou hast given me may be with me, that they may see my glory."* (St. John, chap. xvii. 24.)

Now these words cannot apply to the world, for it is not fit for the kingdom of heaven, unless it be first purified; as a man covered with dirt and mire, would not .be fit to enter the chamber of a king. But God loved the world, and delivered his Son for it, that he might cleanse it, and make it fit for his kingdom. Wherefore Christ prayed for his enemies, not that they might remain in their wickedness, but that his Father might pardon them, and thereby cleanse them, that so they might not be of the world. This our Saviour observed in his prayer, when he said, ***"Not for the world do I pray," for he added a little lower, " That the world may believe that thou hast sent me." The conclusion, therefore, is, Christ prayed for his friends, not for the world, because unless we first leave the world before we leave the body, we cannot arrive at the kingdom of God.***

Wherefore, whoever loveth this heavenly city, let him hasten to depart from the world, lest the last day suddenly come upon him, and he be snatched from life, when there will be no hope of his salvation. And when in spirit he shall have left the world, let him forget it and its pleasures, and remember continually the city of the Lord alone, vowing with the prophet David: ***"If I forget thee, Jerusalem, let my right hand be forgotten. Let my tongue cleave to my jaws, if I do not remember thee: if I make not Jerusalem the beginning of my joy."*** (Psalm cxxxvi.)

This is a true mark of being citizens of the eternal city, if truly from our heart we prefer rather to be deprived of our tongue and of our hands, than to do or say any thing against the love of God our Father, and our heavenly country: and if "the beginning of our joy " be indeed that City, which maketh its inhabitants so blessed as not to take pleasure in any earthly happiness, and the mere remembrance and expectation of future joys, be alone sufficient to gladden our heart in this our exile.

We will now conclude this book with a passage from

St. Augustine, that those who may not perhaps believe my words, may at least credit those of so great a man. In his Explanation of the 61st Psalm, he mentions what are the true marks of the citizens of the world, and of the inhabitants of the city of God: ***"All who seek after earthly things,"*** he saith, ***" all who prefer the happiness of the world before God, all who mind their own interests, and not those of Jesus Christ, belong to that city which is mystically called Babylon, and have for their king, the Devil; but all who mind the things that are above; who meditate on heavenly truths; who live in the world with fear lest they should offend God, and who when they do offend him, are not ashamed to confess their sins; the mild, the holy, and just, and good, all these belong to that city which hath Christ for its King."***

BOOK III

ALL THE BLESSED ARE THE FAMILIAR SONS OF GOD.

" I REJOICED at the things that were said to me: We shall go into the house of the Lord." (Psalm cxxi.)

That good and faithful servant has abundant and unspeakable cause to rejoice, who hath either diligently laboured in the vineyard, or multiplied his talents in business, or was the first to win the prize in the race, or who hath gained a crown in a war or single combat, who hath carefully fed the flock entrusted to him, and courageously defended them from the wolves: and now having completed all his labours, he enters with joy into the house of his Lord.

But let us consider why that is called a House which before was named a city: it is not because the house is narrow, and therefore doth not deserve the name of a city: on the contrary, it is infinitely more extensive than any city or kingdom. Hear how the prophet Baruch exclaims: *"O Israel, how great is the house of God, and how vast is the place of his possession! It is great, and hath no end: it is high and immense"* (chap. iii. 24.)

But why is the House so great? The first reason is, because the blessed although occupying every part of the kingdom of heaven, are all the familiar friends and domestics of God. For if mention were only made of a kingdom or city, it might be supposed by some, that there would be many in the city of our God, who could never see him, never speak unto him, except they gained admittance by other greater saints. But this is not the case; for all behold God always; they hold converse with Him, they speak with Him face to face whether seraphim or cherubim, apostles or prophets, or inferior angels and saints.

Of our angel-guardians who belong to the last order of spirits, our Lord saith: ***"Their angels in heaven always see the face of my Father who is in heaven."*** And St. Paul, writing to the Ephesians, tells us, that all the blessed are not only citizens of the saints, but also "domestics of God." Wherefore, their habitation is not only called a city, but likewise a "House" There are many mansions in heaven, some high, some low; there is also a diversity of crowns, some great, some inferior, according to the degree of merit: but yet all the citizens are blessed and happy, and all clean of heart, and full of charity.

Wherefore, every one in that House sees God, and converses with him as a domestic and friend; although in earthly kingdoms and cities, there are many who can never see the king, and very few who are admitted to his friendship, or to an interview. Another reason appears to be, because although in a city many do see the king and speak to him, yet all are not his sons and heirs, but only those who live in the palace, and are acknowledged to be his sons and heirs.

But in the kingdom of heaven and in the city of our God, all the saints, without any exception, are true sons of God, brothers of Christ, heirs of God, and co-heirs with Christ: neither do the great despise the inferior, nor is there any envy or jealousy amongst them.

And when our Lord taught us to recite daily the *"Our Father,"* he therein excluded no one: and when he will say at the last day, "Come, ye blessed of my Father, possess you the kingdom, prepared for you from the foundation of the world" he will not exclude any one of the just: and when the Apostle said to the Romans, *"Whosoever are led by the Spirit of God, they are the sons of God;" and again, "For the Spirit himself giveth testimony to our spirit, that we are the sons of God. And if sons, heirs also; heirs indeed of God, and joint heirs with Christ,"* no one is excluded, neither great nor little, provided he possess the Spirit of God, and suffer himself to be led by him.

This is also given to all who have been regenerated in Christ, and who shall persevere in faith, hope, and charity. St. Peter also, in his first Epistle, promises to the regenerated *" an inheritance incorruptible and undefiled, that cannot fade, reserved in heaven." In fine, St. John in his Epistle says to all the Just, without exception: " Behold, what manner of charity the Father hath bestowed upon us, that we should be called, and should be the sons of God." (chap, iii.)*

Justly, therefore, is the habitation of the blessed called a House and not merely a city and kingdom, wherein all are sons and heirs of our great King, and all beloved by Him as his sons, and by Christ as his brothers: with reason may they exclaim with the prophet: *"How good and pleasant is it, for brethren to dwell together in unity."*

What greater happiness can be conceived, than to converse with innumerable angels, to be loved by them with a most sincere love, to be treated as a brother, to be embraced as a brother!

THE MAGNITUDE AND BEAUTY OF THE HOUSE OF GOD.

ANOTHER reason may be assigned, why the habitation of the saints is called a House, because it has especially if the abode of royalty ornaments, consisting of halls, chanibers, and other apartments, which a city does not possess.

For who can number the carpets, tapestry, pictures, precious vests, and gold and silver vessels which adorn the palaces of kings? And not only the interior decorations are of a great value, but the building itself also is admirable, on account of the precious marble, the pillars, the gilded or painted courts, the hanging gardens, and other things which it would be too long to enumerate.

After Solomon, king of Jerusalem, had built a temple to the Lord of suitable magnificence, he also erected a palace for himself of such extent, that the building thereof took thirteen years; though at the same time he employed many men, and had at hand an abundance of precious stones and cedar- wood. With the same expense and industry, he built a palace for his wife, the daughter of the king of Egypt, and the house ***"of the forest of***

Libanus," of which a description is given in the third Book of Kings: and so sumptuous was it, that it seems incredible.

Wherefore, when the sacred Scripture calls that the House which before it had called the city of God, the meaning is, that both the city and the kingdom shine as resplendent as a royal palace doth shine. For the prophet Baruch hath told us, ***" the house of God is so great"*** (Baruch iii.24) that it occupies the whole extent of the kingdom of God.

If a whole kingdom possessed as much magnificence as its chief city, this would indeed excite our admiration. Who will not therefore be astonished, when he recollects that the kingdom of heaven is called the House of God because all the beauty and value of its ornaments are the same, as the house of God itself? Justly doth the prophet David exclaim: ***"My soul longeth and fainteth for the courts of the Lord." (Psalm lxxxiii.)***

Who will not then desire with his whole heart, to see and to possess this royal and most noble palace, which equals in its extent a whole kingdom? And, on the other hand, to see and to possess this boundless kingdom, which equals any royal palace in beauty and magnificence? But not only would our souls desire such a house and such a kingdom, were it attentively to consider, and faithfully believe these words; but it would even be quite ravished by the consideration of the beauty and magnitude thereof.

But alas! being solicitous for earthly goods, we deem those objects alone great, which we see on earth, and therefore we think not of invisible things: we act just as children do, who never having left their fathers house, love it beyond all others, and never think of the palaces of kings; or like rustics who have never visited any great city, they are solicitous only about the cultivation of the fields, about the repair of their thatched cottages: but no cares ever disturb them about palaces, towers, forums,

theatres, honours, dignities, riches, or splendid banquets. And, perchance, these rustics and children are
more happy than rich citizens and great princes, because
those things which appear grand, bring with them more
trouble and danger than solid utility and dignity.

But the good things in the heavenly House of God
our Father, are both truly great and cause no trouble
unto us, nor danger: they will free us from every evil, not
for a time only, but for ever and ever.

Wherefore, St. Paul saith, who was neither a child
nor a rustic, who had known the goods of this world,
being a most learned man, and intimate with the Wise;
who had been in the house of God, and had visited the
heavenly city, being rapt into paradise and the third
heaven he saith of himself: ***"While we look not at the
things which are seen, but at the things which are
not seen. For the things which are seen are temporal;
but the things which are not seen, are eternal;" and
again: " Our conversation is in heaven ....Seek
the things that are above, where Christ is sitting at
the right hand of God. Mind the things that are
above, not the things that are upon the earth."***

THE CHAMBERS IN THE HOUSE OF GOD.

THERE is another reason why the kingdom of heaven is called the house of the Lord: it is derived from these words of our Master, **" In my Father s house there are many mansions. "** In earthly dwellings there are dining-rooms, couches to sleep on, and halls or courts for various purposes, which cannot be performed outside the house. Now in the house of the Lord there are many chambers, wherein all the saints not only feast on royal banquets, but what is most wonderful, and not possible to be credited, had not the Holy Spirit revealed it to us, the King himself ministers unto them, being girded!

Thus our Lord speaks in St. Luke: **" Blessed are those servants, whom when the Lord cometh he shall find watching. Amen I say to you, that he will gird himself, and make them sit down to meat, and passing will minister unto them. "** (chap. xii. 37.)

What a banquet is this, I ask thee! Who ever heard of such a feast? The Lord stands, the servant reclines; the Lord is girded, that He may " minister " without impediment, the servant is ungirded, that he may recline more freely; the Lord passeth bringing food, the servant eateth with pleasure the royal food!

O! did we but consider and understand these things, how insignificant would all earthly pleasures become! Our Lord on one occasion girded himself with a towel, that he might wash the feet of his disciples. But Peter was astonished, and could not endure to see his Lord wash the feet of servants. - And with reason was Peter thus astonished, because he beheld majesty humbling itself to give an example of humility.

But in our celestial house, this ministering of the Lord is not a humiliation, but a favour; for the servants of God in heaven, where the proud will not enter, stand not in need of an example of humility, for all are confirmed and made perfect in every kind of virtue. Wherefore the "girding" of the Lord signifies, that He will as freely and as readily be a Lord unto each one of his servants, by loading and refreshing them with every blessing, as if He had nothing else to do, and were alone with each one of them!

O Christian soul! what doth this mean? Would that thou wert wise, and couldst understand with what honour and joy the Lord will fill his servant for ever! If these truths could descend deeply into thy heart, truly thou wouldst become fervent in spirit; and with thy loins girt, thou wouldst joyfully devote thy whole being to the service of so sweet a Lord.

And if any one of his poor brethren met thee, not only wouldst thou not despise him, or look angrily at him; but with the bowels of charity enlarged, thou wouldst relieve him and nourish him, mindful of these words: ***"Amen I say to you, as long as you did it to one of these my least brethren, you did it to me."*** (St. Matthew, xxv. 40.)

Where it is said, "He will make them sit down to meat" signifies, that the blessed being now admitted into their Father's house, can sit down without the least danger or solicitude, and enjoy all the good things with which the house of the Lord is filled. From henceforth, no one will be able, either by force or by fraud, to hinder them or forbid them enjoying every good most freely. Lastly, where it is said that, ***"passing he will minister unto them,"*** this signifies, there is a special banquet for the saints in the Lord himself, for he is the bread of life; he is the fountain of wisdom; he is a hidden manna, which no one knoweth of but he that receiveth.

Wherefore, He passeth unto all, he giveth unto all ineffable banquets, that satiate without loathsomeness, and fill without satiety.

ON THE COUCHES IN THE HOUSE OF GOD.

*L*ET *us now pass from the chambers to the couches. " The saints shall rejoice in glory," saith David, "they shall be joyful in their beds." (Psalm cxlix.) These "beds" signify nothing more, than the eternal rest of the saints, and that " sleep " of which the prophet speaks in other places, "When he shall give sleep to his beloved ;" behold the inheritance of the Lord," &c.*

And again, *"In peace in the self same I will sleep, and I will rest." In fine, this is that rest of which St. John makes mention; "Write, blessed are the dead who die in the Lord. From henceforth now, saith the Spirit, that they may rest from their labours; for their works follow them"* (Apocalypse, chap. xiv. 13.)

Great is this blessing, possessed only by the saints; for in this life no one is entirely free from labour, and those who seem at rest, such as nobles and rich men, are often oppressed with the greater troubles. Not without reason hath our Lord compared riches to thorns, in the parable of the sower; and Job saith; *" Mans life upon earth is a warfare," and one of his companions: "Man is born to labour and the bird to fly."*

But Ecclesiasticus is the clearest of all on this point: *"Great labour is created for all men, and a heavy yoke is upon the children of Adam, from the day of their coming out of their mother's womb, until the day of their burial into the mother of all. Their thoughts, and fears of the heart, their imagination of things to come, and the day of their end: From him that sitteth on a glorious throne, unto him that is humbled in earth and ashes. From him that weareth purple and beareth the crown, even to him that is covered with rough linen: wrath, envy, trouble, unquietness, and the fear of death, continual anger and strife."* (chap, xl.1-4)

Thus Ecclesiasticus most beautifully teacheth us, that no mortal can enjoy "rest" at any time. But I will briefly explain these words, that all may understand how great is the "sleep", that is, the rest of the blessed. " Great labour is created for all men, and a heavy yoke is upon the children of Adam." Occupation is opposed to rest: but because many are occupied in pleasant things, in hunting, in games, in music, in dancing, it is added " A heavy yoke," to show us that he speaks of laborious and troublesome labours with which no one is pleased, and which all fly from. But these troublesome labours are " created for all men," that is, destined for men from their creation, as their individual and inseparable companions.

This Ecclesiasticus explains, lest perhaps he might not be understood by some, " From the day of their coming out of their mothers womb, until the day of their burial in the mother of all." Wherefore, oxen that sometimes bear a heavy yoke, but rest at night, are better off than man who is compelled to carry his " heavy yoke " day and night.

He then briefly mentions a part of the troublesome occupations, which like unto a most heavy yoke, press upon the neck of mortals. ***"Their thoughts and fears of the heart, their imagination of things to come, and the day of their end."*** The first portion of their labour is the thought of the future, for they are always solicitous about tomorrow, saying within themselves, What will happen after this? Shall we lose the little we possess? " From this solicitude proceeds a continual fear, which does not suffer man to be at rest.

This solicitude, with its offspring, which is fear, is two- fold: one which the mind imagines to itself; the other which is certain, and which one can avoid. Of the first Ecclesiasticus speaks, Their imagination of things to come :" of the latter, " The day of their end." Men imagine, that is, represent to themselves various future contingencies, which no less disturb them than if they were certainly to happen. But the thought and fear of death especially frightens them, which is called "the day of their end :" all await this with so much terror, that St. Paul in his Epistle to the Hebrews, calls it a continual " servitude :" for the expectation of death can embitter all the pleasures of life. Lastly, Ecclesiasticus adds, that this laborious occupation is so common to all the sons of Adam as to be long to all men, from the first unto the last; ***"from him that sitteth on a glorious throne, that weareth purple and beareth the crown, unto him that is humbled in earth and ashes."*** Thus all men, since the. sin of Adam, are more miserable even than the beasts of the field: for these live without fear, and are not solicitous for tomorrow, neither do they remember past labours, nor are they disturbed by the imagination of things to come. And therefore hath Ecclesiasticus said, that this yoke is upon " all the children of Adam," in order that he might both exclude the beasts of the field, and show us that the cause of all this misery, was the sin of our first parent.

But the lot of those who aspire not after their heavenly home is the most miserable of all, because, after having carried a heavy yoke in this life, they will be forced to bear a still more heavy one in hell. In this world our troubles are often united with some consolations; but in hell there will be labour and sorrow, without rest or consolation: for, in the blessed House of God alone can there be rest without labour, and consolation without sorrow. With reason doth the prophet say: *" The saints shall rejoice in glory: they shall be joyful in their beds." (Psalm cxlix.)*

They rest not as those that sleep, who do not feel their rest, but they rest with great "joy," knowing and feeling with eternal gratitude their most happy rest, free from labour, pain, fear, and trouble.

Truly, if there were nothing else in the House of the Lord but this eternal rest, would it not be worthy of being purchased by all the sorrows and labours of this life? and if in hell there were no other torment but an everlasting want of rest, would it not be worthy of being redeemed by the daily prayers and tears of a whole life?

As it will be consoling to the saints to behold, at their departure from this world, the end of all their labours and sorrows, so, likewise, will it be bitter for the wicked to reflect, at their death, that henceforth they can hope for no rest from their sorrows.

Death is said to be the chief of all terrible things; and yet, because it appears to bring some rest, therefore most miserable are they who shall descend into hell, for *"They shall seek death, and shall not find it: and they shall desire to die, and death shall fly from them"* (Apocalypse ix. 6.) Wherefore, the being deprived of all rest will be a more grievous evil than even death itself. And yet, so great is the blindness of men, that they think nothing of losing eternal rest, and of descending into that pit wherein their torments will never admit of consolation.

ON THE COURTS OF THE HOUSE OF GOD.

IN earthly houses certain places are set apart for various purposes. But, in the courts of the blessed, all are occupied in one occupation alone, the praise of their great King. Here, in this world, some are occupied in gaining money, in acquiring dignities, in acquiring knowledge, either to teach or to learn; whilst others devote themselves to mechanical arts, in order to provide the necessaries of life. But amongst the living, immortal inhabitants of heaven there will be no wants, no ignorance, no necessity, no ambition: all being content with their state, neither desire nor require anything more - they are entirely devoted to the enjoyment, love, and praise of their *" chief Good."*

But some one may say, that the duty of praising God in psalms and hymns, and especially in reciting the canonical hours, is laborious and tiresome; and some there are who even consider it a heavy burden imposed upon them to spend so much time in singing in the Churches, and in praising God. To whom we answer, that "praising" God in this life is a meritorious act, but in the next it will be a reward. Hence it is, that what may be to many laborious here, in heaven will be a sweet occupation to all the saints. Now, we read and sing many things which we do not understand, whilst we labour much in driving away vain thoughts, which are like so many troublesome flies. Moreover, our body, which is mortal, cannot for any long space of time attend to the functions of the mind without being fatigued. But, in our blessed country, the body will be immortal and impassible; vain thoughts will depart; we shall most perfectly understand what we sing; and, what is the greatest of all, the divine "praise" will be nothing more than the exercise of our happiness.

Wherefore, if eternal happiness will not be troublesome, neither can the eternal praising of God be. That the praising of God is an exercise of beatitude, the prophet teacheth us: ***"Blessed are they that dwell in thy house, O Lord: they shall praise thee for ever and ever"*** (Psalm lxxxiii.5) As beatitude consists in always loving and beholding the " chief Good" so the exercise of beatitude consists in always admiring and praising God; and as no one will be wearied in loving Him, so no one will be wearied in praising Him. And again: we shall not only not grow weary in seeing and loving God, but we shall never be tired in seeing and praising the works of God, which will always be before us, showing forth His wonderful beauty, Nor can we praise the beautiful works of God without our praising the Author of them at the same time, for they will ever cry out unto us: ***"He made us, and not we ourselves."***

In fine, as we can never forget the benefits with which God hath loaded us, so we cannot but exult with the most grateful hearts in the praises of our most bountiful Benefactor.

Let us then conclude with St. Augustine, and say: ***"What else could be done, where neither any sloth will be admitted, nor any want shall labour? God Himself will be the end of our desires: He will be seen*** *without end, loved without weariness, praised without fatigue. This gift, this love, this exercise, will be truly shared by all, as eternal life itself will be common to all. There we shall rest and see: we shall see and love: we shall love and praise. Behold, what will be in the end without end. What other end have we than to arrive at that kingdom which hath no end?"(De Civitate Dei, cap. 30)*

ON THE FIRST GATE OF THE HOUSE OF GOD, WHICH IS FAITH.

HAVING explained these points, it now remains for us to consider what is the gate by which we shall be enabled to enter that most blessed House. But our Lord Himself, in the Gospel, not only makes mention of the gate, but also tells us that it is very narrow, for, being asked, ***"Lord, are they few that are saved?"***

He answered: ***"Strive to enter by the narrow gate, for many, I say to you, shall seek to enter, and shall not be able. But when the Master of the House shall be gone in, and shall shut the door, you shall begin to stand without, and knock at the door, saying: Lord, open to us. And He shall say to you: I know not whence you are: depart from me, all ye workers of iniquity."*** (St. Luke, chap, xiii.) Thus our Lord plainly teaches us, that the "gate" of the house of God, which is in heaven, is very narrow, although the House itself is most extensive; and that, because it is narrow, many will not enter therein who otherwise would; that they indeed desire to enter, but will not strive for it, nor be willing to suffer any violence.

But we will explain how it is that the gate of this most extensive House is narrow. The gate has four divisions the threshold, the inner court, and two side passages that is, four stones: one below, another above, and two at the sides; which, in our gate, are four virtues, essentially necessary in order to enter the heavenly house. These are faith, hope, charity, and humility. Faith and hope are the two lateral stones, charity is the inner court, humility is the threshold on which we walk. But all these stones that is, all these virtues have their length and breadth so small, that in themselves they are narrow, and, accordingly, they make the gate very narrow.

Let us begin with faith. True Christian faith is so narrow that, unless the mind do violence to itself, and suffer itself to be reduced as it were into captivity, to be bound and trampled upon, no one can enter by it. This is what St. Paul means in his Second Epistle to the Corinthians: ***"Bringing into captivity every understanding unto the obedience of Christ."*** (chap, x.) The Christian faith proposes many things to be believed, which are so beyond all understanding that it is most difficult to give our con sent to them; and yet are we commanded to believe them so firmly that we should be prepared (if necessary) to die a thousand times rather than deny one article of faith.

This is a difficult duty, and no wonder so few comply with it. This is the reason why so many go over to Mahometanism and other heresies, because they cannot bear the strictness of faith, but have made the gate very wide, which nevertheless leads, not to life, but to destruction, according to the words of our Lord in St. Matthew: ***"Wide is the gate, and broad is the way that leadeth to destruction, and many there are who go in thereat."*** (chap, vii.13) Every one naturally desires knowledge, but all do not readily assent to a proposition, unless it be demonstrated, or a probable reason for it be given. St. Paul, the Apostle, experienced this; for, although he eloquently preached from an infused and acquired learning, and by the gift of tongues, yet when he spoke of the Resurrection of the dead many laughed at him, and. others said, " What is it that this word-sower would say?" And when he preached " Christ crucified," it appeared foolishness to the Gentiles, and to the Jews a stumbling- block, as he mentions in his First Epistle to the Corinthians. Hence, the ancient heretics, in order to widen the narrow gate, invented various errors.

Some denied the mystery of the Trinity, as the Sabellians and Arians; others the mystery of the Incarnation, as the Nestorians and Eutychians; others the Resurrection of the dead, as the Origenists, &c. But all these gates [1] being built by human architects, and wanting a solid foundation, fell in a short time, so that now we scarcely know their names: and these even would not have reached us, had we not read them in the works of those who exposed them, as St. Ireneus, Philaster, St. Epiphanius, St. Augustine, Theodoret, &c.

The Mahometans, whose sect is now so widely extended, have cast away nearly all the most difficult points in the Christian faith the blessed Trinity, the Incarnation of the divine Word, the death and resurrection of the Son of God, the sacrament of Penance, and the holy Eucharist. These being thus cast aside, the gate is widened to admit an innumerable multitude.

But the heretics of our own time have endeavoured to enter by another way, for they have taken away those narrow barriers which relate not so much to the understanding as to action. The Christian faith teaches that all sins are to be avoided; that we shall have to give an account even of every idle word; that if we fall into mortal sin, we must confess it to a priest, and blot it out by serious contrition and satisfaction; that good works, though laborious and difficult, are to be performed if prescribed by our superiors; that the kingdom of heaven can be acquired by good works, as a crown of justice, and a reward of labour; that " celibacy" is to be observed by priests; that monks and nuns are obliged to keep their vows.

These and other points, which make the gate narrow, the heretics have so taken away as to make it very wide. For they assert, that " faith alone is necessary for salvation, so that a Christian could not perish, though denied with every sin, provided only he believed; that there is no need of confessing our sins to a priest, but only to , God; that contrition is not required, a certain terror of the mind being sufficient; that works of penance and satisfaction are not necessary; that a priest is at liberty to marry, and monks and nuns to Violate their vows; that superiors cannot oblige the faithful to perform good works, &c. These and other doctrines of faith being taken away, the heretics made the gate of salvation very wide for themselves: but they opened a way that leadeth to destruction, and through it they brought to perdition, together with themselves, an immense multitude of foolish men.

But neither do all Catholics keep within the narrow boundaries of faith, for, although they believe what their faith teaches them, yet because they live differently from what their faith commands, they are proved to be in the number of those of whom St. Paul speaks where he says: " They profess that they know God, but in their works they deny him." Thus, these likewise enter in at the wide gate that leads to destruction. Wherefore, with regard to faith, when our Lord was asked, " If they are few who are saved? " we answer, few there are; and hence all must strive to enter in at the narrow gate.

ON HOPE, WHICH IS THE SECOND GATE OF THE HOUSE OF GOD.

HOPE likewise has its difficulties, whether we consider the greatness of the reward promised, or our own weakness and nothingness. If an ignorant rustic, without experience were commanded to hope that in a short time he should possess the wisdom of Solomon, or that of Plato and Aristotle, and at the same time the kingdom of Alexander the Great or of Augustus how, I ask, could such an humble individual be persuaded to hope for such great things?

But this is much more easy than that a mortal man could hope to possess the wisdom and power of the angels in heaven, who are pure intelligences. For this rustic, and Alexander, and Aristotle, were of the same nature, and alike mortal; and the wisdom of Aristotle did not exceed all human wisdom, neither did the empire of Alexander occupy a third part of the globe. But Christians are commanded to hope for an equality with the angels, according to the words of our Lord: *" But they that shall be accounted worthy of that world, and of the resurrection of the dead, shall neither be married nor take wives. Neither can they die any more:*

for they are equal to the angels, and are the children of God, being the children of the resurrection" (St. Matthew, chap. xx. 38.)

Again: if a man that crawls upon the ground were commanded to hope that in a short time he would fly through the air, or subsist in the water for some time, and go here and there, how could he be induced to believe these things? And yet large birds, as cranes and storks, fly through the air as swiftly as eagles; and large ships, heavy laden, sail up and down the waters just as the pilot directs them. But Christians are without doubt commanded to hope, that with their bodies they will one day ascend above the heavens; and that from heaven to earth they can descend without the least danger of falling, and contend with the sun itself in its course from east to west, with the certain hope of victory. In line, if some poor orphan were commanded to hope that he would be adopted as a son by a great king unknown to him, truly it would take much labour to induce him to think this could be possible; and yet both are men, children of the earth, and doomed to die.

But Christian hope teaches us, that every one, provided he be baptized in Christ, and observe his commandments, will have the spirit of adoption" from God, will be truly chosen His son, and made heir of all things which God Himself possesseth co-heir with Christ, who is His natural and only Son, and whom the Father hath appointed Heir of all things.

If these great and sublime hopes were entertained by Christians as they should be, they would certainly make them fearless as lions, so that no dangers or terrors could conquer them; and they would exclaim with the prophet: " The Lord is my keeper: I will not fear what man can do unto me If armies in camp should stand together against me, my heart shall not fear ;" and with the apostle: "I can do all things in Him who strengtheneth me;" and again: " If God be for us, who shall be against us ?"

But few there are who hope for such aid as they ought; whilst many are found who do not look even for temporal blessings from God, but trust more to their own cunning, to theft and lies, than in the aid of the Most High. Our Lord Himself, in St. Matthew and St. Luke, admonishes the faithful by most beautiful parables, not to be too solicitous about food and raiment, because our heavenly Father, who nourishes the birds that neither sow nor reap, and clothes the lilies of the field that neither labour nor spin, will much more take care of His children for whom He intends an eternal kingdom: but yet, so little confidence have many people in God, that often in their troubles they rather have recourse either to human fraud or diabolical arts, than to the Almighty. Wherefore, if these do not hope to receive from God what He gives to the birds of the air, and the lilies of the field, and which He hath, promised to give them if they trust in Him, this is a great proof that their hope is not of that character which belongs to the sons of God, who hope to receive a share in His eternal kingdom.

And since no one can attain salvation without a certain and living hope, which is a part of the gate of the heavenly " House" therefore few are they that are saved.

There are also other and greater difficulties in the virtue of hope. It commands us to despise present things, which are seen, and to hope for future goods, which are not seen; to give alms to the poor, that, being multiplied, they may be returned to us in heaven, though no one here can see them, or conceive what we shall there receive, if we sow them on earth. A rustic can indeed be easily persuaded to sow his seed in the ground, because the experience of many years teaches him that what is sown with labour will be reaped with joy. But no experience teaches us that what is given to the poor will be received back again with interest in heaven.

Therefore, it appears difficult to men to lose present things, which are seen, and to hope for future blessings, which are not seen.

Lastly, it is an evident proof that a firm confidence in God is a very narrow gate, to behold such a great number that weep, lament, murmur, blaspheme, and despair. Those who confide in God, He either takes away from them their afflictions, or gives them patience, united with such great consolation, as to enable them to exclaim with the Apostle: ***"I am filled with consolation, I superabound with joy in all my tribulations."*** They, therefore, that immoderately weep and lament in their troubles, prove as St. Basil shows in his Explanation of the 45th Psalm that they may exclaim in words: ***"The Lord is our refuge and our strength ;"*** but that few truly and earnestly say so in their hearts.

ON CHARITY, WHICH IS
THE THIRD GATE.

LET us now speak of charity, which is the court of the heavenly gate. Charity is the queen of virtues, and on one side seems boundless, because it extends to God, to the angels, to men even those who may be unknown to us, and our enemies; but, on the other side it is made **"narrow,"** on account of the incredible difficulties it brings along with it, since its precepts are to be observed, not only in word and in tongue, but **"in deed and in truth."** For what, I ask, doth this queen command? First, that we love God **" with our whole heart, with our whole soul, with our whole strength."** We are reduced to great difficulties when we endeavour to fulfil these commands.

For, to love God with our whole heart and strength, what else is it but a true and earnest love? "With our whole heart and soul" signifies, that our love must be real, not feigned; not in word and in tongue, as St. James saith, but in word and in deed. With our whole strength" signifies, that our love of God ought to be supreme. The force of the precept, therefore, consists in loving God with a true and perfect love, so that we should prefer nothing before Him, but be prepared with the patriarch Abraham, if the glory of God required it, to sacrifice our only begotten and most beloved son.

And not this merely; but also, as our Lord commands us in the Gospel, to hate father and mother, wife and children, brothers and sisters, even our own soul, and to renounce all that we possess: that is, we should be ready to be deprived of all these things with such promptitude as we should have, if we hated them in reality.

This is truly a severe command, and who can understand it? But how easily will men be found, and these not a few, who would rather renounce God and his promises than their riches and temporal honours, and much less their life or that of their sons! St. Cyprian, in his Treatise on the *"Lapsed"* beareth testimony, that in the primitive Church, when the fire of charity was much more ardent than now, there were many deserters, who preferred their riches and their lives before God; and Eusebius, in his Ecclesiastical History, testifies the same.

But what shall we say of charity towards our neighbours? What doth charity command us to do with regard to our neighbours? That we love them as we love ourselves; and that what we wish to be done to ourselves, we do to our neighbours also. Who therefore is there, being much in need, would not wish the rich to give him something out of their superabundance?

Neither would he consider it as an excuse, if the rich man answered, *"That he was encumbered with debt, that he had purchased a villa at an enormous sum, that he was building a sumptuous palace, or, at least, adorning it with precious marble."*

But these were perhaps not necessary, and therefore charity does not allow our indigent neighbours to be deprived of subsistence. On this point I beseech the reader to consult St. Basil in his "Sermon" to the rich; and also St. Bernard on the words: *"Behold, we have left all things."* He will see, and be terrified at the danger of those who do not think they will have to render an account to God of their riches, but live according to their own pleasure, not according to the will of God, and in charity towards their neighbours. If we shall have to give an account of ***"every idle word,"*** much more shall we of money ill-spent.

But let us hear St. John the apostle, and from him learn how extensive is the duty of charity. He saith: ***"In this we have known the charity of God, because He hath laid down His life for us: and we ought to lay down our lives for the brethren."*** (1 Epist. chap. iii. 16.) Christ laid down His life for His servants: can it, therefore, be a great thing if we lay down our life for our brethren? The apostle does not say we can, but ***"we ought to lay down our life for the brethren;" neither did he say, I think, I advise, but absolutely, "We ought."*** And if we ought to give our life, why not our riches much more? Wherefore, St. Gregory justly concludes: ***" Since our soul, by which we live, is incomparably superior to our earthly substance, which we possess, who will not give his substance when he ought to lay down his life?"***

The same may be said on other points; for he who ought to lay down his life for the brethren, ought much more to pardon an injury or an affront. And ought he not also to be on his guard, lest he injure his brother in word or in deed? But, because this precept of charity towards God and our neighbour is so difficult that few comply with it; therefore, when our Lord was asked, ***" If few are saved," with reason did He answer, "Few:" we must then endeavour, with our whole strength, to enter with the few the narrow gate.***

ON HUMILITY, WHICH IS THE FOURTH GATE.

THERE now remaineth humility, which also hath its difficulties, and these not a few. What doth our Master command, who hath most truly said of Himself: ***"Learn of me, because I am meek and humble of heart", "Go, sit down in the last place?"***

When He came into this world, he was born in a stable, and died on a cross. Truly, no one, when born, could have found a more lowly place; nor, dying, a more disgraceful one. And whilst He lived, He was poorer, not only than men, but even than the beasts of the field: for the foxes had holes, and the birds of the air their nests, ***"but the Son of man had nowhere to lay His head." But what means, " Sit down in the last place?" This is the meaning: wherever thou art, however great thou mayest be, always consider thyself worthy of the last place. St. Paul, in his Epistle to the Galatians, gives a reason for this where he says: "If any man think himself to be something, whereas he is nothing, he deceiveth himself." (ch. vi. 3.)***

He did not say, he who thinks himself to be great, or

superior to others, either in wisdom, or power, or virtue; neither did he say, if any one think himself not to be great, or superior to others, but only equal to them; he said, *" If any man think himself to be something." In fine, he did not say, since he is poor, or unlearned, or ignoble, but, "Whereas he is nothing."*

Thus the apostle could not descend lower, in order to designate the *"lowest place,"* and to give a worthy explanation of the words of our Lord. But it may be said, it is necessary that men should be in high stations such as, prelates, princes, kings, emperors, and pontiffs. Be it so: but yet each one ought to sit down in the lowest place, until the Lord shall say, *" Ascend higher."* Of this St. Augustine gives us an illustrious example, which I will mention in his own words: *"From these that love the world I have separated myself: with those who govern the people I have not considered myself equal, nor at the banquet have I chosen the highest place, but the lower: but the Lord said unto me, "Ascend higher" But so much did I fear the episcopacy, that I would not have approached it, since amongst men the fame of a certain name had spread; and in this place I knew there was no bishop. I was on my guard, and endeavoured, as far as possible, to be saved in an humble situation, not to be in danger in a high one. But, as I have said, the servant ought not to contradict his Lord."* ("De Vitâ Clericorum")

Oh, that all men would imitate such an example! we should then have many good prelates, many good princes, many excellent magistrates. But, because many push themselves for ward, not waiting for a vocation from the Lord, the Almighty is oftentimes angry; and for an example to others, He compels many to sit down in the lowest place, that all may learn how honours and riches, as well as spiritual blessings, depend on Him alone. Hence, we frequently see very rich men reduced in a short time to extreme poverty, and great princes cast down from their thrones.

But it is not sufficient to wait for a vocation from God; but we ought also, in the prelacy or sovereignty, not to be over wise, but, according to the advice of the Wise man, the more we are elevated, the more humble should we be unto all: not in demeanour, but in heart, as St. Gregory teacheth in his pastoral, and St. Augustine more clearly in his 109th Epistle: ***"Let your dignity" he saith, "be honourable before men; but, before God, place it under your feet."***

Each one ought to think others better, and therefore higher than himself. For he is properly and truly the greatest, who is the greatest in the sight of God; and he is the greatest who is the best; and he is the best who excels in virtue, whatever may be his dignity, riches, titles, &c.

Virtue alone makes a man good, not dignity, riches, or titles; and if virtues make a man good, greater virtues make him better, and the greatest make him the best. And they who possess virtue in a higher degree excel all others. Now, we may know that humility is one of these great virtues, because our Lord Himself says: "He that shall humble himself shall be exalted," which words the blessed Virgin follows in the Canticle: "He hath scattered the proud in the conceit of their heart, and hath exalted the humble." And St. Peter saith: " Be you humbled, therefore, under the mighty hand of God, that He may exalt you in the time of visitation;" and St. James: ***" Be humbled in the sight of the Lord, and He will exalt you." In fine, St. Paul says of Christ: "He humbled Himself, and therefore hath God exalted Him."***

Since, therefore, these virtues, and especially those of charity and humility, make men good before God; and since again, no one truly knows what he is in the sight of the Almighty, or what others are or will be therefore, it is dangerous to prefer ourselves to others, but most useful to humble ourselves before all men. Wherefore, our Lord absolutely saith: ***"Sit down in the lowest place."*** But how many comply with this divine precept? For what do men contend more than for precedence? What labours do those endure who endeavour to reconcile men that quarrel about a point of honour! How many do we often hear using these words of Scripture, ***" I will not give my honour to another ?"*** And yet the Most High speaks thus in Isaiah, to whom alone such words belong. God alone ought not to be humble, since humility is the virtue that restrains a man from desiring to ascend above himself, but since God dwelleth in the highest heaven, nothing can be above Him. Wherefore, pride is intolerable, because a worm of the earth dares to say, ***"I will not give my glory unto another"***.

And yet, these same worms whom pride so swells that they say with God, " I will not give my glory to another," humble themselves as to acknowledge they are the slaves of honour that is, of a false esteem. And so faithfully do these serve their master, honour, that they rather prefer to be cruelly slain in single combat, and to descend into hell, [1] than suffer any affront to be given to the idol of their honour. vanity of vanities! Oh, how much doth this smoke of honour blind the eyes of the soul! And yet we call ourselves Christians, and know that Christ heard from His enemies: ***"Behold a man that is a glutton and a wine-drinker Thou art a Samaritan, and hast a devil. This man casteth not out the devils but by Beelzebub the prince, the prince of devils ;"*** and yet no one heard Him exclaim, ***"Thou art a liar"*** but, because He was meek and humble of heart, ***"Who, when he was reviled, did not revile: when he suffered, he threatened not: but delivered himself to him that judged him unjustly."(1 Peter ii.23)***

From these considerations, it is manifest that the "gate" of life is narrow, both on account of humility, as well as of the theological virtues, faith, hope, and charity: "Few" enter this gate; and therefore, when the question is asked, **" _If few are saved"_** most truly must we answer, "Few;" because few there are who endeavour, with their whole strength, to enter in at this narrow gate.

MORE CONSIDERATIONS ON FAITH.

BUT lest we should seem, by too much severity, to drive men away from entering the gate, I will show [1] that the "gate" which on one side appears most narrow, on account of the perfection of virtue required; on the other is very wide and easy to enter, by reason of the omnipotence, truth, and mercy of God, if we be truly desirous of entering it.

Let us begin again with faith. Faith certainly proposes for our belief mysteries most difficult, far above our reason and understanding, and sublimely exalted even above the natural capacity of the angels themselves. But since the doctrine of faith admonishes us, that these mysteries are to be believed on the authority of God, who cannot deceive, and not on that of angels, or of men, then the bounds begin to be enlarged. If faith said, ***"Believe in one God, and three persons; believe that the Son of God was born of the blessed Virgin; believe that Christ rose immortal from the dead on the third day by His own power: believe all these points most firmly because SS. Peter, Paul, and John, Isaias, Jeremias, and Ezekiel, have said so "I should*** *hesitate, not daring to believe men like myself on such difficult subjects. It is said, "Every man is a liar;"* and therefore it is that we require oaths and witnesses, before we put our trust in men. But since faith says, *"All these things hath God revealed; and neither Peter, nor Paul, nor John, nor the other apostles and prophets, taught them on their own authority, but learned them from God; and since they preached His word, not their own, then my heart enlargeth itself, and is prepared to believe."*

And that it was God who spoke by the apostles and prophets, hath been manifested unto us by Him in so many signs and wonders, that it would be foolish and rash not to believe. Thus speaks the apostle to the Hebrews: *" Which having begun to be declared by the Lord, was confirmed unto us by them that heard Him. God also bearing them witness by signs and wonders, and divers miracles, and distributions of the Holy Ghost according to His own will."* (chap, ii.) What God says, who will gain say? God cannot lie, for if He could, He would not be God.

But these mysteries, which are proposed to our belief, are above our reason. They are: but they are not above the power and wisdom of God. Therefore, saith St. James, *"God is greater than our heart;"* because He can do what we cannot understand, and His essence and existence are more elevated than our mind can comprehend. If an unlearned man easily believes the many incredible things philosophers and astronomers mention concerning the magnitude of the sun and of the planets, why should not man readily believe also whatever God hath deigned to reveal, since there is an infinite distance between the wisdom and power of the one, and the small spark of reason with which the other is endowed? They therefore, who consider these remarks, will find no difficulty in believing what the Church proposes.

MORE CONSIDERATIONS ON HOPE.

WE may say the same of the virtue of hope: for if what we hope to receive in the life to come, were said to depend on the promises of man, justly should we be rejected as vain impostors, because men can both deceive, and are quite unable to give such great rewards.

But we say, they are not to be hoped for from man, but from God, who can neither lie, since He is truth, nor deceive us, since He is goodness: nor is anything impossible with Him, since He is omnipotent. Wherefore, justly would that rustic think himself mocked at, were anyone to promise him the wisdom of Solomon or the power of Augustus, because he that would promise such things would be a man, deceitful and weak. But ought not a Christian to hope, to whom God promises eternal life, the kingdom of heaven, and a paradise of every pleasure?

Perhaps we want pledges of this bountiful intention of God. But, as a figure of present things, did not God lead His people through a dry path across the Red Sea? Did He not rain down upon them manna from heaven?

Did He not conduct them by Josue into the promised land? Should such a remarkable figure be considered vain and useless?

Moreover, if "God so loved the world, as to give His only-begotten Son" hath He not "with Him given us all things?" That which we hope to receive from God, is it not excelled by the " gift" which He hath given to us, when we neither hoped nor asked for it? If He hath given to sinners and to His enemies the death of His Son, will He not give to the justified and to His friends the life of the same divine Son? But, not content with this, the Holy Spirit is added as a pledge of our inheritance. He crieth in our heart, "Abba (Father); and giveth testimony to our spirit, that we are the sons of God; and if sons, heirs also heirs indeed of God, and joint-heirs with Christ: yet so, if we suffer with Him." (chap. viii. Epistle to the Romans.)

Wherefore, if the magnitude of the things promised seems beyond our hopes, yet they cannot exceed the power of the Promisor; and since this power is infinite, it can easily strengthen our hopes, that we shall without doubt receive the promises. And this promise God hath confirmed with an oath, as the apostle proves in his Epistle to the Hebrews: so that by two certain things, .by the promise of Him who cannot be, joined to an oath, we can rest our hope, as on a safe Anchor, of approaching even within the veil where Jesus hath entered for us, being a priest for ever according to the order of Melchisedech.

OTHER CONSIDERATIONS ON CHARITY.

BUT what shall we say of charity? It is very narrow, on account of the difficulty of fulfilling its precepts; but, because of the divine goodness, to which it directs us, it may be said to be very wide. For why should it appear difficult to love God with our whole heart, and. soul, and strength, since He is most beautiful, most wise, and most worthy of infinite love?

It is not difficult to love that which is excellent and beautiful on the earth; but it is not to love. Doth God, then, seem to do us an injury when He so strictly commands us to love Him, as if we were not bound to love Him of our own accord?

We ardently love what is beautiful in the world, because we clearly see it, but ***"God no one hath ever seen" Thus we do not see God, but we daily behold His works, which are so beautiful, and of which the Wise man speaks: "With whose beauty if they, being deceived, took them to be Gods, let them know how much the Lord of them is more beautiful than they: for the first Author of beauty made all these things." (ch. xiii. 3.)*** We also experience His goodness in His daily benefits to us; and we have Him for a testimony who beholds us, and who cannot deceive: viz. the Holy Spirit, who speaks by the apostles and prophets in the holy Scripture. ***God, therefore, is so good and beautiful, that He alone deserves to be called good and beautiful.***

But you will say, it is hard that we should, for the love of God, be sometimes compelled to lose our property, friends, and even life itself. I acknowledge that it is so to those who love not God: but to those who do love Him, and desire to possess Him, I assert that it is very easy, especially since, if we despise temporal goods for the love of God, we shall possess those that are incomparably superior to them.

And what are these? You lose corruptible riches, but you will acquire an eternal kingdom; you lose father, brothers, and friends, but you will possess God for your father, Christ for your brother, and all the angels and saints for your friends and companions: you lose a temporal life, full of misery, but you will gain an eternal one, full of happiness. Hear the Canticle of divine love: ***"If a man should give all the substance of his house for love, he shall despise it as nothing;" and a little above: "Many waters cannot quench charity, neither can the floods drown it." Hear, again, a lover of God; "Who then shall separate us from the love of Christ? Shall tribulation? or distress? or famine? or nakedness? or danger? or persecution? or the sword? But in all these things we overcome, because of Him that hath loved us." (Epistle to the Romans, chap. viii. 35.)***

But so to love my neighbour as to share my goods with him; and, even though he were my enemy and had grievously injured me, I should be obliged not only to pardon him, but also to be kind towards him: this seems to be against nature. It may be against nature corrupted by sin, but not against nature regenerated by the grace of Christ. Does not God himself share His blessings with His enemies, and daily pardon them, and return them good for evil? ***"He maketh His sun to rise upon the good and the bad, and raineth upon the just and the unjust."***

Now, if God thus acts towards His enemies, it is not against the nature of God, nor the nature of men created after His image, to love his enemies, and do them good. But it is opposite to the nature of beasts, and of those, ***"who, when they were in honour, did not understand; but they are compared to senseless beasts, and are become like to them."***

OTHER CONSIDERATIONS ON HUMILITY.

I NOW come to humility, which, like its other sisters, is hard to be acquired by the proud and the arrogant; but to those who attend the School of Christ and wish to learn of Him, it is very easy of attainment. And first, we should humble ourselves **"under the powerful hand of God,"** as St. Peter admonishes us, and his co-apostle St. James confirms.

But what difficulty can there be, in a mortal man humbling himself before his Immortal and Omnipotent God? Secondly, we should choose the last place amongst men, because "each one should esteem others better than them selves" as the apostle tells us in his Epistle to the Philippians. They who know themselves and are conscious of their own infirmities, and know not those of their neighbour, find no difficulty in esteeming all others before themselves, and conceding them a higher place. For as pride springs from ignorance, so does humility from a knowledge of one's self. The heart of the proud man easily sees the vices which others have, because they are all outside him; but his own vices, often very numerous, he sees not, because they are within him; just as the eye does not behold what is within, but only what is without.

Of this the Pharisee is an example for us, who gave thanks to God, that he was not as the rest of men a thief, unjust, an adulterer. He did not observe these vices in himself; but there were others concealed within; pride, blindness of soul, and impenitence which he did not see; therefore he preferred himself to the publican praying in the same temple. But the publican, who had better eyes, saw his own faults, and not his virtues; therefore he sat down in the lowest place, and standing afar off, struck his breast, imploring the mercy of God: by His judgment, the one went home justified; the other condemned. Wherefore, if we seriously endeavour to know ourselves, we shall find no difficulty in entering the "gate" of the House of the Lord.

But to all this we must add, that the gate which appears so very narrow, and almost impenetrable, to those who are heavy and corpulent, or covered with many garments, or that attempt to enter with an erect body; this same gate is broad and wide to those who enter unencumbered, naked, and lowly. Wherefore, we are to blame, if we cannot easily enter at the same gate, through which so many saints have before us, without any difficulty or trouble.

Begin then, Christian soul, to cast aside the burden of riches: remember that your riches have been given you by God, as to a steward, not as to a master, in order that you should distribute them amongst the poor, but not to hoard them up carefully for yourself alone; and thus your soul being free from the love of riches, having thrown aside as it were a great burthen, will easily enter the " narrow gate." Cast away also a love of carnal pleasures, or rather cast out those noxious humours that produce wind, and inflate the body. In fine, reject the opinion of your own excellence; put on the humility of Christ; bow down your neck to the obedience of His commands, and then complain, if you cannot easily enter in at the gate of salvation.

THE NECESSITY OF ENTERING THIS GATE, HOWEVER NARROW, IF WE WISH TO BE SAVED.

BUT whether this gate be broad or narrow, we must necessarily strive to enter by it: for after this life, which passeth as a shadow, there is no other place where we can well remain, except within this gate. Therefore our Lord admonishes us, saying, ***"Strive ye to enter in at the narrow gate,"*** because, as He adds in the same place, those who remain without, will all be banished to a place where there will be eternal weeping and gnashing of teeth: these signify the greatest torments with a despair of any remedy; and thence comes a madness that impatiently endures what it does not wish to endure, and will always be compelled to endure.

But how much better is it to strive to enter in at the narrow gate, where rest and joy will be found, after we have borne a little labour and sorrow? If indeed men could escape the narrowness of the "gate, and the pains of hell at the same time, perhaps their frailty might excuse them from using violence to enter.

But since we are compelled, either to labour here for a time by doing violence, or to fall hereafter into eternal sorrows, what judgment what reason can we have that would induce us to avoid minor evils, and so to find those that are intolerable and most grievous! But even if no evils would follow after this life, but being deprived of the House of God, where alone are eternal joys, this ought to induce us to strive to enter, not only through the narrowness of the gate, but through briars and thorns, and fire and the sword.

And though during this life we cannot feel what a loss it is to be deprived " of beatitude, yet after the separation of the soul from the body, the eyes of the mind will be opened and will most clearly see what a loss, what an infinite loss it is, not to have obtained the end for which we were created. This desire is signified by those words which are mentioned in the Gospel, as being used by those who shall remain outside: "Lord, Lord, open unto us"

The desire of their last end will ever torment these wretched beings, and the remorse of conscience will never rest: thus the words will be fulfilled, *" Their worm will never die, and their fire shall never be extinguished."*

Oh! if we could now seriously think with what ardour these men will then exclaim, "Lord, Lord, open unto us:" as if they said, we cannot live without entering into the House of the Lord, and yet we cannot die! Wherefore we exist not to live, but to be for ever miserable. Wherefore *" open unto us," because we are prepared to suffer everything, provided only we can enter. But He will answer: " I know you not."*

The year of jubilee has ended; when you could have entered, you would not; now therefore it is but just, that when you wish to enter, you cannot." Thus though deprived of all hope, they will never cease exclaiming, being impelled by a natural desire, *" Lord, Lord, open unto us."* But because in their lifetime they were deaf to the exhortations of the Lord crying out to them, *" Strive ye to enter in at the narrow gate,"* now

*the Lord will turn a deaf ear to them exclaiming, "
Lord, Lord, open unto us." Wherefore, if we be wise,
let us now consult our own welfare whilst we have
time: let us do now, while we are able, what we shall
then wish to have done, and shall not be able to do it.*

BOOK IV

TRUE JOY IS TO BE FOUND IN HEAVEN.

PARADISE is a name of pleasure and delight, for it signifies a garden, or most beautiful orchard, suitable both for recreation and amusement. In the book of Genesis this paradise of pleasure is not once named, when the terrestrial paradise is the subject of the discourse.

But in the prophet Ezechiel speaking of the heavenly paradise, it is said of the chief angel who afterward fell and became the devil: Thou wast in the pleasures of the paradise of God.*" But since the Holy Scriptures mention nothing of Paradise, but that there were in it many trees and the fountain of living water, therefore it is my intention under the word " Paradise," to explain the joys and pleasures which the blessed possess in heaven. And this will be, unless I am deceived, a useful contemplation to excite our minds to seek and reflect upon the things above: and thus so to regulate our life, that when we depart hence, it may not be to sorrow and darkness, but by the divine assistance, to Eternal light and happiness.*

All men, with few exceptions, are influenced more by

pleasure, than by any thing else. And the Church in one of her prayers says, *" There may our hearts be fixed, where our true joy is."* And first we shall consider what the Holy Scripture says of the heavenly Paradise, whence we shall prove that in it are true joys; then we shall endeavour to explain what these joys are: and lastly, by various reasons, or rather comparisons, we shall prove that these joys are far more excellent than we can either comprehend, or think, or even imagine.

First, then, the name of paradise signifies pleasure and delight, as we have already seen from the Book of Genesis. And that there is a Paradise in heaven, Ezechiel testifies. Our Lord also testifies in the gospel, when he said to the thief hanging by him: *" This day thou shalt be with me in paradise"* He used the word paradise for the kingdom of God, and its essential beatitude: for the good thief had said, *" Lord, remember me when thou shalt come into thy kingdom."* St. Paul testifies in his second Epistle to the Corinthians, where he says, *" I know a man in Christ Such a one rapt even to the third heaven, and was caught up into paradise."*

St. John testifies in his Apocalypse, where he introduces the Lord thus speaking: *" To him that overcometh I will give to eat of the tree of life, which is in the paradise of my God."* From these passages it is evident, that the region of the " blessed " is a place of happiness and delight. And when our Lord says to the good and faithful servant, *"Enter thou into the joy of thy Lord" does He not most clearly declare, that the house or city of God is a place of joy, to which good and faithful servants are admitted when they leave this world?*

Our Lord in many places compares the kingdom of heaven to a supper, as we read in St. Luke, where it is said: *"A man made a great supper," & c. And again, "I dispose to you, as my Father hath disposed to me, a kingdom: that you may eat and drink at my table, in my kingdom." And when likewise we are told in the Apocalypse, "Blessed are they that are called to the marriage supper of the Lamb."*

The Scripture, by the figure of the supper, certainly points out the pleasure and delight of the heavenly paradise; unless some one assert, that there is no pleasure in the sense of taste. In addition to these passages, the kingdom of God both in the Gospels and the Apocalypse is compared to royal nuptials: as we learn from the parable of the king, who made a marriage for his son; and from the parable of the wise and foolish virgins, of whom the wise went with the bridegroom to the marriage; but the foolish virgins remained without. The same also is found in the Apocalypse, where many things are said of the " marriage supper of the Lamb" celebrated with great magnificence in the kingdom of heaven. Now the beatitude of the saints may be compared to a royal marriage, because on such occasions every variety of pleasure is experienced and enjoyed. But of this we shall treat in the following Book.

In fine, in the Apocalypse St. John sees a choir of virgins who followed the Lamb wheresoever He goeth, and sang a new canticle which no one else could sing. Which passage St. Augustine explains in his Book on " Holy Virginity" as having relation to certain joys and holy pleasures, which virgins alone will enjoy. Thus it is manifest, that in our heavenly kingdom and city, there are many true joys amid most abundant pleasures.

ON THE JOY OF THE UNDERSTANDING.

SINCE it has been proved from Holy Scripture, that in the kingdom of heaven there is true joy, we will now explain what those joys are. And first, we will briefly explain the joys of the Understanding, of the Will, and of the Memory, which relate to the mind: afterwards the joys of the other senses which relate to the body. We do not here mean to assert, that the understanding, memory, and the senses of the body are the proper seat of joy; sincere are not ignorant that joy as well as desire, properly belong to the will in the superior part, and to the appetite in the inferior.

But we speak as men generally do- who hesitate not to say, ***"The eye is delighted with the beauty of colour, and the ear with the harmony of sound"***

By the joy of the understanding, therefore, or of the memory, or external senses, we mean the pleasure which men experience from those objects, which they either understand, or remember, or derive from their external senses.

The chief joy of the " Blessed" then will be, to behold with the eyes of the soul God face to face, as St.

Paul mentions in his first Epistle to the Corinthians: and to be hold Him as He is, according to St. John. And how great this joy will be, we can conjecture from what the prophet Isaias and the apostle Paul testify, ***that it exceeds all the joys which we have seen, or heard, or desired, or can imagine: "Eye hath not seen, nor ear heard, neither hath it entered into the heart of man, what things God hath prepared for them that love Him"*** (1 Corinth, ii. 9.)

The holy Scripture also speaks of a particular and essential happiness which consists in seeing God according to the words of our Lord: " Blessed are the clean of heart, for they shall see God :" and also: ***" Now this is eternal life: that they may know thee, the only true God, and Jesus Christ whom thou hast sent." (St. John, xvii. 3.)***

This truly seems a great privilege, that no one can see, or hear, or desire, or imagine any good equal to that which the sight of God will convey to us; and yet this is no exaggeration, but the simple truth, because the eyes, the ears, and the heart of man are accustomed to finite and limited joys: but the sight of God is a vision of light inaccessible, of an infinite Good which contains every good, according to what the Lord said to Moses when he had asked, ***"Show me thy face."*** He answered, ***"I will show thee every good thing."*** But that we may prove this from reason, we learn from St. Thomas that delight which comes from knowledge requires three things power, a sensible object suitable to that power, and an union of the object with this power; and that in proportion as the power is capable of knowledge, and the object more noble, and the union more intimate, so much the greater pleasure is derived.

But no one can doubt but that the mind is much more pure and noble, and more capable of knowledge than the exterior senses. Now, all must admit that God is the highest and most noble object, placed not only above all objects of sense, but also above those of the mind, being infinite Goodness itself. But it is also equally certain, that a union of the mind with God by a clear vision is so intimate that the essence of God will penetrate the whole soul, whilst the soul herself will be transformed into God as if she were plunged into a great sea.

Who, therefore, can imagine the greatness of this joy? The sweetness of this embrace from an infinite Good, from a Spouse of infinite beauty? From the beautiful union of colour with the sense of sight, and the sweetest sounds with the sense of hearing, we certainly experience great pleasure; and often it is so great, that many by it almost lose their senses. And yet the sense of feeling is material, and common to us with beasts: the objects also are corporal, and deceive us as often as they delight us. In fine, the union is superficial and external; and in many of the senses it is not an union of the object itself, but of its image with the mind. But the spiritual union of God with the understanding is more firm, durable, and complete; whilst corporal pleasures that are derived from the senses, because they are mutable, cannot be durable nor complete, being given to us as it were by drops. Wherefore, without doubt, the pleasure of the mind is greater than that of the senses.

Wherefore, Man! recollect thyself, and weigh impartially the pleasure which the world offers thee, with that which God offers thee, when He promises Himself to those that love Him: choose what thou wishest for. If thou love pleasure which is certainly pleasing to thee, thou wilt choose the greatest, rather than the least; the ever-enduring, rather than the momentary. But not only the sight of God is promised to the good in heaven, but also the sight of all those things which God hath made. Here on earth we perceive by our eyes the sun, moon, stars; the sea, rivers, animals, trees and minerals. But our mind does not know the substance of these created things, their essential difference, their properties or power: we cannot see even our own soul, but like blind men we feel for effects, and by reasoning, acquire a little knowledge. What then will be the joy, when our mind in the vision of God, will clearly see the substance of all things, their difference, properties and power! And what great exultation will be ours, when we shall behold the innumerable army of angels, not one of whom resembles another, and shall clearly see the difference of all! What unbounded joy will it be, when we shall behold those holy men, who have been from the beginning of the world even unto the end, united together with all the angels! When we shall behold the merits of each, their crowns and palms of victory!

We shall also see with feelings of pleasure, the crimes and torments of the damned, in which the sanctity of the good, and the justice of God will wonderfully shine forth; for then the just will wash their hands in the blood of the wicked, as the prophet saith. And what doth "washing their hands in the blood of the wicked" signify, but that the good works of the blessed will shine more Brightly, in comparison with the works of the wicked? The virginity of some will be more resplendent, when compared with the adulteries of others: and the fasts and alms-deeds of many, when compared with the gluttony and revellings of others.

It will then be said: this young man was beautiful, and yet he observed perpetual chastity: this other youth was beautiful also, but not content with his own wife, he often committed adulteries and sacrileges. This man was rich and of noble extraction, and yet he fasted and prayed often, and gave abundant alms: another was equally rich and of noble extraction, but being addicted to gluttony and drunkenness, he spent his money in pleasures, so that he had nothing to give to the poor. Hence it will be, that the joy of the Just will be increased, by knowing the crimes of the wicked. At the same time, their joy will also be great, from the contemplation of the justice which will be so conspicuous, in the rewards of the blessed and the punishment of the wicked.

Now, in human affairs, we perceive a great anomaly, because crime is often united with reward, and virtue with punishment, so that the justice of God seems in a manner to be obscured amongst men. But then every crime will have its punishment, and every virtue its reward, so that the beauty of God's justice will excite incredible joy in the minds of the blessed.

ON THE JOY OF THE WILL.

THERE are three things which produce the greatest love in the will. One is a most ardent and inextinguishable love of God and of our neighbour; for love is the chief ingredient of every thing loved. He that loves, thinks that every thing which he loves, is most beautiful and excellent; and therefore he rejoices greatly when he sees them; and when absent from them grieves inconsolably. We see parents, who naturally have great love for their children, consider them the most beautiful, talented, and prudent, although they are often deformed and devoid of judgment and knowledge.

And if a choice were given to them, they would not exchange their sons for any others, however superior to their own in the judgment of men. We often, too, behold people, either by chance or any other cause, in love with deformed persons, to converse with whom they consider a great pleasure, and to be separated from them a great calamity. This would certainly not be the case, unless, as we have said, love is the ingredient of everything loved. And since this is the case, how great will be the joy of the saints, to converse with God and all the blessed, whom they will ever love with the most ardent affection, and who not falsely, but very truly, are most beautiful and excellent, and from whom they know they will never be removed.

On the other hand, one of the greatest torments of hell will be, to be united with those whom we shall hold in the utmost horror, and who we know circumvented us with a thousand artifices.

Another circumstance that will cause great joy in the mind of the blessed, will be a certain inexpressible repose, and satiety without fulness, which will make them happy and contented in every way. Here on earth no one is contented with his lot, no one but wishes for more than he has, which he cannot obtain. Hence all are hungry, all thirsty, all live in discontent.

Nor ought this to appear wonderful to us, since our soul is capable of an infinite and eternal good, and created things are frail and insignificant, which cannot last long. What then will be the joy of that man, who shall see himself in a place where he will live quite contented! where he will desire nothing, fear nothing, require nothing, nor seek for anything more! Peace! that exceedeth every pleasure which the world can give, and which alone is found in the heavenly Jerusalem, the city of our great and peaceful King! For thee my soul sigheth, full of troubles and temptations: in the recollection and expectation of thee alone, it resteth for a little time.

The third circumstance that will give joy to the blessed, is perfect justice, and that more perfect than original justice was in Adam. The one subjected the inferior part to the superior, till the latter was subject to God: but the other will subject the inferior to the superior, and the superior to God, by a most firm and indissoluble union. The one was like a woollen or linen vest: but the other will be all of gold or silk, which will make the will most beautiful and lovely to God, to itself, to the angels, and to all the blessed. This is that perfect justice which hath no stain, not even a venial one; so that of such a soul clothed with such a garment it may be said: *"Thou art all beautiful, my be loved, and there is no spot in thee."*

This includes all those virtues which admit of no imperfection, and how great joy and pleasure this justice brings with it, the wise man beareth witness in the Proverbs, *"A secure mind is like a continual feast." (chap, xv.) That mind alone is secure, whose conscience never stings, and which by perfect justice is so established in good that it cannot fall, even for a moment. Of this St. Paul beareth witness when he says, " The kingdom of God is not meat and drink; but justice, and peace, and joy in the Holy Ghost" (Epistle to the Romans, chap. xiv. 17.)* Here the holy Apostle plainly teaches us, that the kingdom of heaven possesses in itself great joy; but that it does not consist in the pleasure of meat and drink, as carnal men might perhaps wish, but in justice, which produces in the mind a solid peace and true joy. For he that is perfectly just, hath not in his heart anything to reprehend him, nor in his actions what others might reprehend. *Hence arises a solid and sweet peace with God, with himself, and with all others: hence, an unspeakable joy in the Holy Ghost, with which no earthly or temporal pleasure can bear any comparison.*

ON THE JOY OF THE MEMORY.

THE memory will supply no small matter for joy, from the recollection of the past. First, the recollection of the benefits of God in the spiritual and corporal, the natural and supernatural life, as well as the temporal and eternal, will bring incredible joy, when the just recollect in how many ways the blessings of heavenly sweetness were given to them. Then the recollection of the dangers from which God delivered them so wonderfully, in every age and every state, will be a source of unbounded joy. And amongst other dangers I consider this the chief, that often they were near committing mortal sin, and therefore near hell, and yet that God, moved by His goodness alone, prevented the sin.

This singular mercy of God being often considered by the elect in their most peaceful kingdom, will give them the greatest delight. And if the saints had not the recollection of these things in heaven, how could they, as the Psalmist saith, sing the mercies of the Lord for ever? *"Nothing will be sweeter in the city"* says *St. Augustine, "than this canticle for the glory of the grace of*

Christ, by which we were redeemed." (Lib. 22. "De Civitate Dei.")

What shall I say of the course of ages from the beginning, even to the end of time? What pleasure will the remembrance of so many vicissitudes bring, of such a variety of things, which the wonderful providence of God so wisely governed, ruled, and conducted to their proper ends! This perhaps is ***"the stream of the river which maketh the city of God joyful."*** What is the course of ages flowing with so great velocity and never interrupting its course, except the stream of the river that rolls its waters continually, till they disappear and are lost in the ocean? And then, whilst the stream floweth and time flieth, many doubt of the providence of God: and some even of His servants are disturbed by this stream of the river which often brings evil to the good, and blessings to the wicked; which takes away the good land from the just, and carries it to the camp of the wicked, and brings them so many temptations, that they seem to complain of the providence of God.

Hear the royal Prophet: " But my feet were almost moved: my steps had well nigh slipped. Because I had a zeal on occasion of the wicked, seeing the prosperity of sinners:" and a little lower: "Behold these are sinners; and yet abounding in the world they have obtained riches. And I said: then have I in vain justified my heart, and washed my hands among the innocent. And I have been scourged all the day, and my chastisement hath been in the mornings." &c. (Psalm lxxii.)

Hear Jeremias: "Thou indeed, Lord, art just, if I will plead with thee, but yet I will speak what is just to thee. Why doth the way of the wicked prosper: why is it well with all them that transgress, and do wickedly? Thou hast planted them, and they have taken root: they prosper and bring forth fruit: thou art near in their mouth, and are far from, their

reins." (chap, xii.) Hear the prophet Habacuc: " Why lookest thou upon them that do unjust things, and holdest thy peace, when the wicked devoureth the man that is more just than himself? And thou wilt make men as the fishes of the sea, and as the creeping things that have no ruler." (chap, i.)

But when the course of time shall be accomplished, and the river shall be lost in the sea, then the saints in heaven, calling to mind all its revolutions, shall clearly read the reason of its vicissitudes in the book of .divine providence, and thereby it is incredible, how the stream of this river represented to them by memory, will make joyful the city of God!

There they will see, why God permitted the first angel and the first man to fall: why the mercy of God liberated man, and did not liberate the angel. There they will see, why God chose for His peculiar people the children of Abraham, who, nevertheless, he foresaw, would be a stiff-necked people: and how great blessings he was preparing, on account of their obstinacy, for the Gentiles. In fine, to omit speaking of His universal providence, there they will see why He permitted many, and nearly all the just, to suffer afflictions; it was, that He might crown them more gloriously. And thus, from the remembrance of them, they will bless with great joy all those crosses which they suffered, since they see them changed into eternal crowns, and they will exclaim with the Prophet: *"According to the multitude of my sorrows in my heart, thy comforts have given joy to my soul."*

ON THE JOY OF THE EYES.

LET us now consider the joys of a glorified body. And first, there will be the joy of the sense of "seeing" which amongst corporal senses is the most noble, and its office the most extensive. This sense then will rejoice at the splendour and beauty of its own body in heaven; for it will see the body reformed by Christ, and made like to the body of His glory as St. Paul mentions in his Epistle to the Philippians.

Nor will its brightness be less than that of the sun, for the Apostle testifies in the Acts of the Apostles, that he saw Christ [1] shining above the brightness of the sun: and our Lord himself in St. Matthew says: ***"Then the just shall shine as the sun in the kingdom of their Father."***

What a glorious spectacle therefore will be presented to the eyes of the blessed, when they shall behold their hands, their feet, and all their members, sending forth rays of light; so that they will no more stand in need of the sun, or of the moon, or of any other inferior light, to dissipate the darkness!

But not only will their own bodies shine as the sun,

but the bodies of all the saints also, and especially the body of Christ himself and of His most blessed Mother.

How doth one sun rejoice at his rising- the whole earth! What then will it be, to behold innumerable suns, most beautiful not only by their brightness, but also by the variety and glory of the members! Nor will the blessed be here obliged to close their eyes, lest they should be injured by the dazzling splendour: for the eyes themselves will be blessed, and therefore made impassible and immortal. For He who will make the eyes of the soul like to His glory, lest seeing God face to face they should be overpowered, will also endow the eyes of the body with impassibility, that they may behold not one sun only but many without injury.

It will also be an addition to the joy of the eyes, as St. Augustine teaches us in his *" City of God"* that the blessed martyrs will display the most illustrious marks of their virtues, in those particular parts of the body in which they endured torments.

What joy, therefore, will it be to see St. Stephen adorned with as many illustrious jewels as he endured blows of the stones in his body! What to see St. John the Baptist, St. James the Great, and St. Paul the Apostle besides others almost infinite in number, who suffered for Christ all shining in unspeakable beauty, more resplendent than any gold! What to behold St. Bartholomew, who was flayed alive, then so glorious beyond the beauty of the richest purple! And, not to mention others, what will it be to behold St. Peter and St. Andrew, and many others who endured the punishment of the cross, now with their hands and feet shining like stars in the greatest splendour!

And with regard to Christ, the King of the martyrs, who for His own glory, and for our comfort, hath deigned to bear the marks of the cross, no tongue can express with what glory these most sacred marks will shine! And all the glory of the saints, when compared with that of Christ, is less than the beauty of the stars when compared with the beauty of the sun.

But what shall I say of the pleasure which the eyes will derive from viewing this most extensive city, which Tobias and St. John, not being able to find sufficient words to express, have described it as adorned with gems and precious stones! What of this new heaven and new earth, which is promised us in the Holy Scripture after the last day? What of the renovation of this whole universe into a better state? For, as these things are unknown to us, so will they delight the eyes of the blessed, when their beauty shall be seen.

ON THE JOY OF THE EARS.

THAT the sense of hearing will be an instrument of speech in heaven, we cannot doubt, for the bodies of the blessed will be truly animated and perfect in every part; such was the body of Christ after His resurrection, which all the apostles, many of the disciples, and many women clearly saw.

They heard Him speaking, and He answered their questions. St. Paul also tells us, that he heard Christ speaking from heaven, and that he answered Him. That there will likewise be "Canticles" sung in heaven, and especially that of "Alleluia" Tobias and St. John testify. From them it is evident, that there will be in that city many most sweet canticles, by which God will be praised, and the ears of the blessed wonderfully delighted. And if everything be in proportion, there can be no doubt but that this canticle will be as sweet and excellent as the cantors themselves are learned, as He who will be praised is so holy, and as the place wherein the canticle will be sung is so glorious, and the choir of hearers so intelligent and numerous! What then will it be amidst a most profound peace, in such concord of mind, and ardour of charity towards their great Benefactor, to hear the most melodious voices singing Alleluia!

If St. Francis, as it is related by St. Bonaventure,[1] was so moved by the sound of a harp touched by an angel for a moment, that he supposed himself to have been in another world, how will our ears be delighted when thousands of harps and cantors shall praise God with most melodious voices! when other thousands, with the like harmony, shall repeat the same canticles again and again! But the praises of God only will not be sung in this city; for the triumphs of the martyrs also, the merits of the confessors, the glory of the virgins, and the victories of all over the snares of the devil, will be celebrated in song: all these praises will redound to the glory of God. Ecclesiasticus says: "*Who hath been tried thereby, and made perfect, he shall have glory everlasting. He that could have transgressed, and hath not transgressed; and could do evil things, and hath not done them: therefore are his goods established in the Lord, and all the Church of the saints shall declare his alms.*" (*chap, xxxi.*)

Now, although these words are to be understood as relating to the praises of those who dwell in the Church on earth; yet nothing prevents us from applying them to the blessed in heaven, and the Church triumphant. For there the saints will have true and eternal glory: there is truly the Church of the saints. And since in the Gospel our Lord saith, that faithful and prudent servants will be praised by God in heaven in these words: "*Well done, good and faithful servant, because thou hast been faithful over a few things, I will place thee over many things: enter thou into the joy of thy Lord;*" what prevents us from supposing that these words of our Lord will be taken up by the whole choir of the celestial city, and most sweetly repeated again and again? The Catholic Church has not hesitated to say of St. Martin: "

Martin, here poor and mean, now rich, enters heaven, and is honoured with heavenly hymns."

In fine, St. Augustine, in the last book of the " City of God" affirms the same in these eloquent words:

" There will be true glory, where no one will be praised, either by the error or flattery of the praiser. True honour will be there, that will be denied to no one who is worthy of it, nor given to any unworthy of it. Nor will any unworthy person aspire to it there, where none but the worthy are admitted." Oh, thrice blessed then will those be, who in this place whence flattery is banished, and where no deceit is found, shall hear their praises sung without danger of pride, but not without an increase of their joy!

ON THE JOY OF THE NOSTRILS.

ON the other senses only a few remarks must be made; not because they will not have great and peculiar pleasures, but because the Holy Scripture does not inform us what these pleasures will be. But this is sufficiently evident, that many bodies of the saints, immediately after their death, began to send forth a most sweet odour, such as no one had perceived before. This St. Jerome relates of the body of St. Hilarion, for he affirms that ten months after his burial his body was found perfect, as if he were still living; and so fragrant was it, that it seemed to have been embalmed. St. Gregory, in his "Dialogues," relates the same thing of the body of St. Servulus, a paralytic. These are his words: "At the departure of his soul such sweet fragrance was scattered, that all who were present were filled with an inconceivable sweetness; and until the body was buried, every one felt the fragrance."

Other examples of a like nature are to be found, both in ancient and modern times. From these cases we may argue, that if the bodies of the deceased saints, after the soul was assumed to glory, breathed such a sweet odour, much more will these bodies breathe the same when they shall be glorified and alive.

St. Gregory in his "Dialogues" also speaks of the body of our Saviour, in the following manner: ***"Then Tarsilla, the virgin, looking up, beheld Jesus coming; and suddenly with such a wonderful fragrance was she covered, that it was a proof to all the Author of sweetness was present."*** And thus, if the glorified body of our Saviour breathed such an odour of sweetness, it is certain that all the bodies of the saints will send forth the sweetest odours: for it is meet that the members should be conformable to their head, not only in their glory, but also in the sweetness of their fragrance. Let those, therefore, who are delighted with odours, think with what sweetness they will be filled, when in that divine garden, adorned with thousands of heavenly flowers, they will inhale such various and sweet odours.

ON THE JOY THE SENSES
OF TOUCH AND TASTE
WILL HAVE.

ON the sense of taste theologians write, that the blessed will not use earthly food; but yet that this sense will have a certain pleasure, lest it should appear to be superfluous; but this pleasure will be suitable to the state and condition of the just. On the sense of touch, all agree that it will be possessed in heaven, since the bodies of the blessed can certainly be touched, being true and animated bodies, according to the words of our Lord: ***"Handle and see: for a spirit hath not flesh and bones, as you see me to have."***

But we do not wish to enter on those points which are disputed in the schools. We believe, however, that the sense of touch will derive no small pleasure from the perpetual beauty of the body endowed with glorified properties, of which St. Paul speaks in his First Epistle to the Corinthians: ***"It is sown in dishonour, it shall rise in glory. It is sown in weakness, it shall rise in power. It is sown a natural body, it shall rise a spiritual body," & c.*** (chap, xv.) , Of these four endowments or privileges of a glorified body, that concerning its splendour relates to the sense of sight, as we have al-

"

ready mentioned; the other three seem properly to relate to the sense of touch.

For as, when the body is attacked with any disorder, or receives a wound which is mortal, it is the sense of touch that suffers; so also, when the body is in health, the same sense rejoices. Greatly, therefore, will the sense of touch rejoice in heaven, when, after the resurrection, the bodies of the blessed will be immortal and impassible, and, consequently, endowed with perpetual health. What would not men give, and especially princes, if, during their whole life, they could be free from the gout, the head-ache, or any other pains?

What then will be the joy in heaven, from which not only death, but every disease and sorrow will be far removed! Wherefore, those endowments by which a corruptible body will rise incorruptible, and that which is infirm will become impassible, relate to the sense of touch. The endowments of agility and subtility, by which what is corporal will be spiritual, seem also to relate to the same sense. It will be a spiritual and glorified body; not because it will not have truly flesh and bones, but because it will be so subject to the spirit, that, by the mere nod of the soul, it will be able without difficulty to move with the greatest velocity, to ascend and descend, to go and to return, to penetrate any place, as if it were not a body but a spirit.

As, therefore, the sense of touch suffers when a heavy body is forced to ascend upwards, or to be moved from place to place quickly; so, on the contrary, it rejoices when the body without labour either ascends or passes quickly from place to place. Behold, then, from what a servitude of corruption the " blessed" will be free, when they will no more stand in need of horses, or chariots, or arms, or servants, or any other thing; but their bodies will of themselves go wherever they wish, and everywhere be free from danger, even in the midst of armed forces.

Would that those who cannot enjoy spiritual delights because they have a vitiated taste, would at least consider these corporal endowments, which are so excellent and desirable, and seek after them! And thus they might be induced gradually to ascend higher; and by these steps, they would at length, by the divine assistance, reach unto eternal joys.

THE JOYS OF HEAVEN COMPARED WITH THOSE OF EARTH.

WE have already explained, according to our ability, what joys are prepared in heaven for those that love God; we will now, by certain external arguments, endeavour to show how great they are. And, first, we shall consider the pleasures which God often gives, even to his enemies, in this life. And truly, so great joys are found in riches, honours, power, and various other pleasures, which God gives to those that even blaspheme Him, or believe not in Him, that nearly all men consider them happy beings. David exclaims: They have called the people **"happy that hath these things"** (Psalm cxliii.)

Who amongst the lovers of this world does not envy Solomon, who reigned forty years, and abounded in riches and every delight, besides having seven hundred wives and three hundred concubines? And yet, according to the opinion of St. Augustine, it seems that he was lost, for thus he speaks: **" Solomon himself was a lover of women, and was cast off by God"** And in his book on the **" City of God"** he says of Solomon what Sal-

lust said of Cataline, "He began well, but ended badly." (In Psalmum, 126.)

St. Gregory also follows St. Augustine in the 2nd Book of his **"Morals"** Not unlike Solomon are, in our own times, the kings of Turkey, Persia, China, and Tartary, who possess the most extensive kingdoms, and are addicted to carnal pleasures; they indulge their heart, their eyes, their ears, and palate in everything they desire.

But not to dwell on these pleasures, which belong only to a few, how great are the joys which God gives to mortals in general, the greater part of whom neither know, nor love, nor fear God! Hath He not given to all the earth with its riches and pleasures, animals, fruit, flowers, and metals? Hath He not given to all men in general the sea, fountains, rivers, and lakes, filled with so many kinds of fishes? Hath He not outspread the heavens, to be as it were the roof of His great house, adorned with innumerable stars? Doth not this same great and most bountiful Lord command His sun to rise and His rain to fall, both upon the just and the unjust?

Now, if He hath given so many pleasures to reprobate sinners and ungrateful slaves, who are deserving of the severest punishments, is it not just that He should reserve for His friends and children joys infinitely greater? Hear St. Augustine: To sinners that blaspheme His name daily, He gives the heavens and the earth: fountains, fruits, health, children, riches, abundance. He who giveth such to sinners, what thinkest thou will He not give to His faithful servants ?"

It is mentioned in the Life of St. Fulgentius,(Apud Surius, Tom. 1) that when he once saw the glory of the Roman senate he exclaimed: ***"O! how beautiful must the heavenly Jerusalem be, if earthly Rome be so glorious! And if in this world so much honour be given to those that love vanity, what honour and glory will*** *be given unto the saints, who behold truth itself!"* St. Augustine, who was such a wise judge of things, does not hesitate to assert there is such a difference between heavenly and earthly joys, that the enjoyment of celestial pleasures for one day only, would be more desirable than the enjoyment of earthly pleasures for thousands of ages.

These are his words: *"So great is the glory of eternal life, that, supposing we could only enjoy it for one day for this alone countless years of this life, full of earthly goods and happiness, should justly be despised; for not without reason has it been said, " Better is one day in thy courts above thousands"* What then shall we say? If these words are true, as they most certainly are, is it not reasonable that we should now at length begin to be wise? Hitherto we have been accustomed to exhort you to despise earthly goods because they are momentary, and to love heavenly things because they are eternal. But now we hear St. Augustine, a most learned doctor, affirming that although earthly goods were eternal, and heavenly ones only momentary, yet that the latter should be preferred to the former! Are we not therefore deaf, blind, stupid, and foolish, if, on account of earthly goods, which are not only vile, but frail and transitory, we despise heavenly treasures, which are most precious and eternal? *Cure, O merciful Lord! our deafness: enlighten our blindness: rouse our stupidity: heal our madness. Why is the light of thy countenance signed upon us, Lord, if we discern not things so great and so necessary? And why hast thou given unto us the judgment of reason, if we see not objects so evident ?"*

THE EARTHLY AND HEAVENLY PARADISE COMPARED.

WE have compared the joys of this world with the joys of the kingdom of heaven: we will now compare in a few words the joys of the earthly paradise, with those of the heavenly one. We may know how great were the pleasures of the terrestrial paradise from this circumstance, that it was a garden of pleasure given to men, who were created according to the image and likeness of God, whilst the other parts of the earth were given to the animals. But when Adam by his sin had lost the honour in which he had been placed by God, and had become like senseless beasts, he was then cast out of paradise into this place.

St. Alchimus, in his poems on Genesis, and others describe paradise as a most beautiful region, and very temperate; where neither the heat of summer could burn, nor the cold of winter injure, but a perpetual spring of flowers flourished, and autumn gave its fruits of every kind. St. Basil thus speaks of it in his book on Paradise: "God planted paradise where there is no violence of wind, no in clemency of seasons, no hail, nor thunder, nor storms; no cold of winter, nor damp of spring, nor summer s heat, nor autumn s dryness: but the seasons are temperate, and in peace among themselves, for they dance around that place; yea, the pleasures of spring, the nourishment of summer, the joy of autumn, and the rest of winter meet there together with their blessings. Clear are its waters, affording great joy to the eye, but possessing more utility than joy. God, therefore, created this place at first as worthy to receive His plants. Afterwards he planted therein a variety of beautiful trees, most pleasing to the sight, and by them He bestowed a most sweet enjoyment"

St. Augustine, in his " City of God," thus speaks of paradise: ***"What could these fear or grieve for, being in possession of such an abundance of good things; where neither death was feared, nor any distemper of the body, and every thing was present which the will could desire; nor could anything enter to injure the body or soul of those that lived so happily? Their love of God was undisturbed, and they lived together in a faithful and sincere friendship: from this love came great joy. There was a tranquil avoiding of sin, which, while it remained, no evil could happen to give them sorrow. How happy, therefore, were these first men, whose minds were agitated by no fears, nor their bodies injured by any evils! The whole human race would have been as happy, had not these committed sin, which they passed to posterity, and had not every one of their descendants sinned, and thus brought damnation."*** So far St. Augustine. I omit others who have written on the wonderful beauty and fruitfulness of the earthly paradise, such as Claudius Marius Victor, St. John Damascene, St. Isidore, &c.

But whatever we may think of these particular accounts, we learn from the Holy Scripture itself that paradise was doubtless a more happy place than this our habitation, since, as a punishment for sin, it was said to Adam: ***"Because thou hast hearkened to the voice of thy wife, and hast eaten of the tree whereof I commanded thee that thou shouldst not eat, cursed is the earth in thy work: with labour and toil shalt thou eat thereof all the days of thy life. Thorns and thistles shall it bring forth to thee,"*** &c. ***And to the woman He said: "I will multiply thy sorrows and thy conceptions; in sorrow shalt thou bring forth children, and thou shalt be under thy husbands power, and he shall have dominion over thee."*** (chap, iii.)

In paradise, therefore, there would not have been sterility of the earth, neither would its cultivation have required labour, nor would it have brought forth briars and thorns; women would always have conceived with fruit, and although they might be subject to their husbands, the subjection would not have been despotic, but mild and moderate. These, therefore, would have led a happy life, without fear or sorrow, without labour and trouble.

Now, if the earthly paradise, had not sin been committed, would have been free from every evil, and have abounded in all good, what ought we to think of our heavenly Paradise, which must be so much more beautiful as it is more excellent, being created for more excellent beings? The heaven of the blessed is, without any comparison, much more sublime than the paradise of Adam; and the blessed inhabitants therein, as they cannot sin or die, are therefore far, far better off than the inhabitants of this earthly paradise, who are exposed to sin and to death.

This, then, being the truth, let us give thanks to God that by the Passion of His Son, instead of the terrestrial paradise snatched from us by the envy of the devil, we have now gained a celestial one, far more excellent than the other; and lest we should be ungrateful to so great a Redeemer, let us strive with our whole strength to enter the heavenly paradise, and to open its gates for ourselves by a lively faith, by a sincere hope, perfect charity, and good works.

THE GOODS OF THIS WORLD, AND THOSE OF THE EARTHLY PARADISE COMPARED WITH THE JOYS OF THE HEAVENLY PARADISE.

WE will now advance further, and compare all the goods of this world, as well as those of the earthly paradise, with the joys of the heavenly paradise alone; and these being united together, we shall see which preponderate. To accomplish this, let us imagine that the riches, power, pleasures, and glory of Solomon, and of other like fortunate men, could be acquired without labour, and retained without fear: let us also suppose, that these men could never sin, nor ever die. These points then being granted, I affirm that the joys of the heavenly paradise alone far excel all the goods of this world and those of the terrestrial paradise united together.

And hence I conclude, that all these joined together can never fill the soul, can never satisfy her desires, because the heart of man is capable of an infinite good: but these are finite. Wherefore, the words of St. Augustine, which are to be found in the beginning of his " Confessions" will always be true: ***Thou hast made us, O Lord, for Thyself; and our heart cannot rest until it rest in Thee.***"[*Fecisti nos, Domine, ad te, et in quietum est*

*cor nostrum, donee requiescat in te." (Confess. Lib.
1. cap. 1.)]*

True also are the words of David, *" I shall be satis-
fied when thy glory shall appear." (Psalm xyi.) But
as long as the heart is not at rest, it will be miserable, and if miserable, it will not be happy. Now, our
heavenly paradise will both satiate the soul, and
take away all fear and uneasiness. For what can he
desire who will be like unto God, because he will see
Him as He is? What can he desire, whom God "shall
place over all his goods ?" What can he desire who
will reign with God, and be a co-heir with Christ,
"whom the Father hath appointed heir of all things
?"* Moreover, because the goods of this world, and those
of the earthly paradise also, may be lost, however great
they are, they are not therefore perfect goods; nor can
they satiate and satisfy the soul; and, on this account,
they cannot make it blessed and happy. But the goods of
the heavenly paradise are, in every way, perfect and secure: they cannot be lost, nor diminished in the least.
For the saints, placed on their most blessed thrones, can
neither die nor sin, and are most certain of their eternal
happiness!

May mortals therefore open the eyes of their soul,
and seriously ponder how important it is, not to lose
their heavenly paradise. The subject is truly of the
deepest interest, and not concerning transitory things;
for the wisdom of God hath said, What doth it profit a
man if he gain the whole world, and lose his own soul ?

ON THE PRICE THAT PARADISE WAS PURCHASED AT, COMPARED WITH PARADISE ITSELF.

THE last comparison will be on the " price " by which Christ purchased paradise for us, and by which we also ought to purchase it with all its goods. Christ, at the price of His blood, purchased paradise for us, which the envy of the devil had snatched from us; not that he might possess it himself, but that he might deprive us of it. For this purpose he seduced Eve, and by her Adam, that he might make them both partakers of his punishment.

Christ therefore is that wise merchant, who sold all that he had to purchase the precious pearl, by which is clearly signified the kingdom of heaven, as He himself teaches, of whom St. Paul speaks: You are bought with a great price;" and St. Peter says, *" Knowing that you were not redeemed with corruptible things as gold or silver .... but with the precious blood of Christ, as of a lamb unspotted and undefiled:" and again, " They deny the Lord who bought them"*

Christ at the same time that He bought paradise, bought us also; for we were captives, and had lost paradise by sin: but Christ redeeming us from our sins, and from the captivity of the devil, made us sons and heirs of God at the same time, and by this means restored paradise to us. Hence, the greatness of paradise is shown to us, by appearing to the wisdom of God worthy of an infinite price. If amongst men, some wise and very rich merchant were to purchase a precious pearl by selling willingly all his goods, certainly no one would doubt but that this pearl was so wonderful and valuable, that scarcely a sufficient price could be given for it.

How greatly therefore ought we to value, if we possess any judgment, the possession of heaven, which the wisdom of God, the Word incarnate, by all his labours, sufferings, and sorrows for the space of thirty years purchased for us, at the price of His most precious death! We must truly be quite senseless, if we sell for the vile value of any earthly goods whatever, that which Christ our Lord deemed worthy of an infinite price.

But not only Christ purchased paradise for us by His blood; all the saints likewise taught by Him, most joyfully gave up whatever they possessed whatever they were worth whatever they were, in order to purchase this same paradise. St. Paul exclaims, ***"I reckon that the sufferings of this time are not worthy to be compared with the glory to come, that shall be revealed in us." (Epistle to the Romans, viii. 18.) But although the blood of Christ was not only a worthy price for paradise, but also (if I may so speak) more than worthy, being supereminent and exceeding the dignity of the thing purchased; yet He wished to purchase us also, that He might honour and exalt us.***

Great is the glory of man, because he can obtain paradise, not only through the merits of Christ, but also by his own merits, which however derive their efficacy from Christ. He therefore that is unwilling to purchase paradise by doing good and avoiding evil, is expelled from the inheritance of Christ, as a wicked and slothful servant in the parable of the Talents. And the apostle seriously admonishes us where he says: ***"And if sons, heirs also; heirs indeed of God, and joint- heirs with Christ: yet so, if we suffer with him, that we may also be glorified with him" (Epistle to the Romans, viii. 17.)***

But lest we should perhaps complain that we have not a worthy price, we must know that nothing is required of us but what we already have. St. Augustine thus speaks: ***"The kingdom of God is worth as much as you possess:"*** he proves this by examples from the Holy Scriptures: ***" What so vile, what so earthly, as to break our bread for the hungry? The kingdom of heaven is worth as much; for it is written, "Possess ye the kingdom of heaven, because I was hungry, and you gave me to eat" "The widow purchased it by her mite: Peter purchased it by leaving his nets: Zaccheus by giving away the half of his patrimony."***

With these words of St. Augustine, Venerable Bede also agrees when he says: ***"The kingdom of heaven requires nothing else but thyself: it is worth as much as thou art: give thyself, and thou shalt possess it." (Serm. 19. De Sanctis.)***

Poor Lazarus had nothing to give but his patience in affliction, and he was carried by angels to Abrahams bosom: the good thief had nothing in this world of his own, besides that voice by which he exclaimed, ***"Remember me when thou shalt come into thy kingdom" and immediately he heard, "This day shalt thou be with me in paradise!"*** truly great is the goodness of God! O! ineffable happiness of man, who can so easily pass over every thing most precious, with the price of his Lord! Dost thou wish, O man! to obtain from God a paradise of every pleasure? Give thyself to Him , and thou wilt possess it. What meaneth " Give thyself?" Love God with thy whole heart: humble thyself under His powerful hand: praise Him at all times: be willing to do His will, whether He wish thee to be rich or poor illustrious or not illustrious in health or in sickness. His will is adorable, and just are all His judgments. ***Say then unto God, I am thine: do with me according to thy pleasure: I do not resist, I do not murmur, I obey thy commands. " My heart is ready, O Lord! my heart is ready. Not my will, but thine be done"***

This holocaust is beyond all value in the sight of God, who standeth in no need of our goods. ***" Doth the Lord desire holocausts and victims," saith Samuel, " and not rather that the voice of the Lord should be obeyed?" This holocaust of obedience Christ daily offered to His Father, according to His own testimony: I do always the things that please Him." And St. Paul, the true imitator of our Saviour, saith: " And therefore we labour, whether absent or present, to please Him." This perfect renunciation of all things we possess, or desire to possess: this denying of one's self in order to please God alone, is the "true price of paradise."***

And he who gives himself in this way to gain paradise, does not lose himself; but most truly finds himself, according to our Lord: ***"He that findeth his life, shall lose it; and he that shall lose his life for me, shall find it."***

But since this truth is hidden from the wise and prudent of this world (who are fools before God ;) and since the number of fools is infinite, therefore "many are called, but few are chosen."

BOOK V

ON THE TREASURE
HIDDEN IN A FIELD.

HITHERTO I have spoken what God hath suggested to me in my meditations, concerning the happiness of the saints, under the names of those places wherein they who are truly happy and blessed dwell; that is, concerning the Kingdom of Heaven, the City of God, the House of the Lord, and the Paradise of delights. I will now add a few remarks on the same subject, under the name of those things by which our Lord hath described the happiness of the Saints, in the parables. But we must first be informed, that these words of our Lord, *" The Kingdom of Heaven is like" & c., which He continually makes use of in the Parables, do not always refer to the words immediately following: as if when our Lord saith, " The kingdom of heaven is like unto a merchant"*

He meant that it was like to this man: the words relate to the whole narration, in which by a similitude the way to the kingdom of heaven is pointed out. And sometimes the happiness of this heavenly kingdom is described obscurely; sometimes clearly, and at other times it can in no way be comprehended. I will explain each part of this division.

When our Lord, in St. Matthew, proposes the parable of the Sower, He describes the fruit which the preaching of the Gospel produces according to the various dispositions of the land, and this is called the **"Mystery of the Kingdom of God:"** but He mentions nothing of the happiness of the saints. But when in the same place, He adds the parable of the cockle, He alludes briefly to the happiness of the saints, when He saith, " The wheat gather ye into my barn, but bind the cockle into bundles to burn." But when in the same chapter He speaks of a merchant seeking good pearls, and of one that found a treasure hidden in a field, He then clearly compares the kingdom of heaven to the pearl and the treasure. I find only six parables of this kind: the first being of the treasure hidden in a field; the second of the precious pearl; the third of the labourers in the vineyard; the fourth of the talents; the fifth of the supper; the sixth of the marriage-feast. To which I shall add two similitudes from the Apostle Paul; one concerning those that run for the prize, the other concerning those that contend in the race. Thus there will be eight **" Considerations"** in the blessed life of the saints, taken from the parables.

The first parable, therefore, [1] makes **" the kingdom of heaven like unto a treasure hidden in a field ;" and it briefly teaches us how it may be acquired, in these words: "Which a man having found, hid it, and for joy thereof goeth and selleth all that he hath, and buyeth that field." (St. Matthew, xiii. 44.)**

A treasure signifies an immense sum of gold, silver, and precious stones; and it ought to be so old, that no memory of it exists, and therefore not having a proper owner, it belongs of right to him that finds it. Now this " treasure" is the Divinity itself, which is hidden in the field of the humanity of Christ, according to the Explanations of St. Hilary, and of St. Jerome in his Commentary on the 13th chapter of St. Matthew; for in Christ, as the Apostle saith, ***are hid all the treasures of wisdom and knowledge.*** " But the Divinity is the truest treasure of all good, and so ancient is it, that no memory remaineth of it, because it is eternal and before all ages: nor had this great treasure ever any owner, since He is himself the Lord of all things. But it is said to belong to those that find it, because He willingly gives it to them, who having sold all their goods, hasten to purchase it. But it is said to be " hidden" in the humanity of Christ, as if buried in a field; because although the Divinity be every where present, yet nowhere is it more so, than in the humanity of Christ, with which it is so united, as to make God and man but one person.

Wherefore the Apostle saith: ***"God was in Christ, reconciling the world to himself."*** And although he was nowhere more than in the humanity of Christ, yet he appeared to be so hidden, that a ***" Light" was necessary to show God was in Christ. This Light was St. John the Baptist, who, as St. John the Apostle writes, " Was a burning and shining light," and of whom David spoke in the person of God the Father, " I have prepared a lamp for my anointed." (Psalm cxxxi. 17.) St. John made Christ manifest, and truly proved Him to be the only- Begotten Son of God, where he says: " No man hath seen God at any time; the only- begotten Son who is in the bosom of the Father, he hath declared Him." (chap. i. 18.) And again: "He that cometh from heaven, is above all;" and a little lower, " The Father loveth the Son; and He hath given all things into his hands. He that believeth in the Son, hath life everlasting; but he that believeth not the Son, shall not see life; but the wrath of God abideth on him." (chap. iii. 35, 36.) But although this " burning and shining light" so clearly proved Christ to be the Son of God; yet the blind***

Jews could not, or would not, acknowledge the Divinity hidden in Christ; for, as the Apostle saith: "If they had known it, they would never have crucified the Lord of glory".

He therefore, who, being divinely enlightened, findeth the treasure, *" hides it, and for joy thereof goeth and selleth all that he hath, and buyeth that field."* To hide the found treasure, is nothing more than under the veil of humility, to conceal the grace we have received; not to be elated by the light given to us from above, nor to boast of our divine consolations and revelations, lest vain glory corrupt our true glory. Wherefore, the Prophet Isaias was accustomed to say, *"My secret to myself;"* and the Apostle Paul, *" If I must glory (it is not expedient indeed): but I will come to the visions and revelations of the Lord. I know a man in Christ above fourteen years ago," &c. (2 Epist. to Corinth, xii.)*

The wonderful revelations he received when rapt into paradise, he passed over in silence for fourteen years; and for ever would he have concealed them, had he not been obliged to reveal them. He plainly says, *"it is not expedient"* to make known such gifts; and under a feigned name he reveals them, to show how greatly it was against his inclination. Something like this happened to St. Francis, when the sacred *" Stigmata"* were miraculously impressed upon him, as St. Bonaventure relates in his life: (Cap. xiii.) he was always accustomed to conceal his divine revelations, and to exclaim with Isaias, *" My secret to myself:"* but yet when he perceived it could not be concealed, he related the whole case with great fear to his inquiring brethren.

With joy to sell all that we possess, and to purchase the field where the treasure was concealed, means that he who wisheth to enjoy God and Christ in the kingdom of heaven, must be entirely free from all affection to temporal things, and deliver himself and all that he possesseth, to the disposal of God; and this he should do, not in sadness or through necessity, but with great joy, for "God loveth a cheerful giver." But he that truly understandeth how great will be the treasure to enjoy Christ in His eternal country; to see with the eyes of the mind His divinity, and with those of the body His humanity, and to be made a partaker of all the good things of God and of Christ, and to possess these securely for ever, to him it will not appear a great sacrifice to despise all temporal goods, and life itself, for the love of God and of eternal happiness. Of this St. Ignatius the martyr is witness, who in his Epistle to the Romans, thus writes: ***"Let fire and the cross; let the companies of wild beasts; let breaking of bones and tearing of members; let the shattering in pieces of the whole body, and all the wicked torments of the devil come upon me: only let me enjoy Jesus Christ."*** (Oxford Ed. 1840. Pg 148)

He that could speak thus, would much less fear want, ignominy, exile, and the prison, in order that he might not lose that incomparable treasure. He therefore who truly desireth to possess the treasure of eternal life, should seriously consider again and again, whether he be prepared to despise all other goods; otherwise he will never obtain, either living or dead, that treasure without which he will be eternally poor and miserable.

But whence is it, that so many anxiously seek after treasures of gold and silver; and not content with human diligence, employ the aid of evil spirits, to the great danger of their life and character? But why do so few seek after Thy treasure, O Lord, my God, who alone canst make men rich, and which can be found without labour, without cost, or danger? I find no other cause, except either the slender faith of Thy people, or their being too occupied in temporal things, which leave them not any time for considering Thy divine promises to men.

Wherefore, dear Lord! increase our faith in Thy promises, and extinguish the thirst of acquiring temporal riches: thus we shall be enabled with greater ardour to seek after Thy treasure; and when found, with Thy especial assistance to purchase it, by selling all our goods.

ON THE PRECIOUS PEARL.

THE next parable, on the precious pearl, is like to the preceding one: this also comes in St. Matthew, (chap, xiii.) In the former was a treasure, and in this is a pearl which may be considered like a treasure. In the former parable, it was necessary by the sale of all our goods, to purchase the hidden treasure; in this one likewise, the merchant sold all his goods, in order to buy it. Wherefore, it will only be necessary to explain in what point this parable differs from the other.

It differs in two things; for in the one a treasure is mentioned, in the other a pearl: and whilst the treasure is accidently found, the pearl is diligently sought for by the merchant. In this parable, the heavenly beatitude, or Christ himself, is named a " pearl," as the holy fathers St. Ambrose and St. Gregory Nazianzen teach. But that which in the preceding parable is called a " treasure" in this is named a " pearl," that we may understand how the divinity of Christ is indeed a treasure, but not divided into many parts of gold, silver, and precious stones, for it is one containing within itself the value of an infinite treasure. A pearl is one substance: but according to Pliny, it contains the essence of all precious things.

Besides, a treasure consists in money alone, in immense sums; and it tends not to pleasure and beauty, but to utility only. Wherefore, lest from the preceding parable any one might suppose, that heavenly beatitude was only useful, and not beautiful nor glorious, our Lord added this other parable; in which He teacheth us, that the divinity of Christ and our happiness are like unto the precious pearl, which, beside the utility of it as a treasure, possesses also the beauty and splendour that adorn and delight us.

I will also remark, that a pearl is a symbol of Christ, both as the Son of God, and as the Son of the Blessed Virgin. For as a pearl is produced by the light of the sun, and from the dew of heaven, as Pliny and others remark; so the Son of God also, as regards His divinity, is begotten of the Father of Light, the uncreated Sun; and therefore we say in the creed, ***"Light of Light, true God of true God*.***"

Again, Christ according to His humanity, was born of the dew of heaven, that is, conceived of the Holy Ghost, not by man. In fine, a pearl is white, shining, solid, pure, light and round. Now, the humanity of Christ, and much more His divinity without any comparison, is white by innocence; shining by wisdom; solid by constancy; pure, because without spot; light, because meek and mild; and round, because perfect in every part. But the pearl is not found by " chance," but is diligently sought after by the prudent merchant. And yet, this parable is not contrary to the preceding one, in which the treasure is said to be found by chance: both are true, but the persons are different: and therefore our Lord, in His divine Providence, joined this parable to the former one, lest we should think all men may find the treasure as it were by chance. Some there are, whom God, by a particular grace, suddenly enlightens, so that neither seeking, nor desiring, nor thinking, they arrive at the true faith and a most ardent charity, and therefore have a certain hope of obtaining eternal life.

These find indeed, as regard themselves, the treasure by chance: but God pre-ordained them to this grace and to future glory, not by chance, but by His eternal Providence. Others there are whom God prevents by His grace, but not suddenly doth He show them the treasure, for He inspires them with a desire of seeking the truth: He makes them careful merchants, and then aids and directs them till they find the precious pearl. St. Paul and St. Augustine are examples in this respect. St. Paul sought not the true treasure which is Christ, but persecuted Him as a seducer, and the Christians as men deluded. And when he was on his journey, "breathing out threatening and slaughter against the disciples of the Lord" our Lord appeared unto him; and at the same time that He blinded the eyes of his body, He illuminated those of the soul with such great light, that immediately he became a preacher, from being a persecutor.

And although this was a fortunate event to him, yet what appeared chance, was in God Providence. For thus he speaks in his Epistle to the Galatians: "For you have heard of my conversation in time past in the Jews religion; how that beyond measure I persecuted the Church of God, and wasted it. And I made progress in the Jews religion above many of my equals in my own nation, being more abundantly zealous for the traditions of my fathers.

And when it pleased him who separated me from my mother's womb, and called me by his grace, to reveal his Son in me, that I might preach him among the Gentiles, immediately I condescended not to flesh and blood." (chap, i.) Wherefore, St. Paul was separated from the womb of his mother by Divine providence, that he might preach the Gospel of Christ; yet he did not seek this precious pearl himself, nor the treasure in the field; but the treasure was offered to him, and he became so much in love with it, that he spared no labours; yea, he endured every danger, and counted all things as dung, that he might gain Christ." On the other hand, St. Augustine began from his youth to burn with a desire of finding the " precious pearl," that is, true wisdom and eternal happiness. But when he fell into the sect of the Manichees, long and greatly did he labour, complaining to himself and disputing with others, that he might discover the truth of the Christian religion.

But when he had discovered in that sect nothing but fabulous and lying accounts, he then almost despaired of finding the truth having spent many years in seeking it. Thus he speaks in his Confessions: (Lib. vi. Cap. i.) I had come into the depth of the sea, and despaired of finding truth. But yet it pleased God that he should at length discover the ***precious pearl:*** and then without any delay, having sold all things that is, having rejected carnal desires by which he was strongly bound, and despising honours and emoluments, to which he ardently aspired, [1] he gave himself up for ever to the service of God alone. This therefore, is the reason, why in the first parable our Lord compared the kingdom of heaven to a treasure found without labour, and by chance; but in the other likened it to a pearl, sought after by a merchant, with great labour and diligence.

It now only remains that the Christian soul, removing aside for a time all other occupations, should seriously consider with in herself, and before God, what is the nature of this business how useful, and how easy it is at the present time; but how difficult, or rather how impossible it will become, if worldly things occupy the attention.

Truly, the children of this world would not omit the opportunity of purchasing a pearl which could be sold for many thousands of pounds. And shall the children of light be so imprudent as to refuse to purchase the " pearl" which will make them eternally rich and happy, and when they will neither be compelled to receive money in usury, nor to travel here and there to seek a purchaser, but it will be quite sufficient willingly to give what they possess, even if they had but two farthings.

Wherefore, O Lord my God, let Thy light shine in my heart: grant that I may know the worth of Thy invaluable pearl, and at the same time the littleness of the price which is required of me to purchase it. Add, Lord, to thy mercies, that thou mayest not in vain show unto me so precious a pearl; and Thou who hast said, ***"Cast ye not your pearls before swine/ grant by Thy grace that if at any time I have been like unto swine, ignorant of the value of Thy pearl, and preferring the husks before it, I may now, enlightened and instructed by Thee, discover the pearl, and selling all my goods, purchase it with joy.***

THE LABOURERS IN THE VINEYARD.

THE third parable follows, concerning the ***"penny a-day,"*** promised by the house holder to those labouring in the vineyard. This parable comes in St. Matthew (c. xx.) and, at first sight, the reward of eternal life appears to be greatly lessened in it, since what before was likened to a treasure and a precious pearl, is now compared to ***" a penny a-day."*** But this comparison is used that the reward may agree with the toil and labour: for the similitude would be inappropriate if a great treasure, or a pearl, or sceptre, or royal diadem were promised to those labouring in the vineyard but for one day.

But it can easily be proved, that the "penny" does not consist in the value of a few brass coins, but that it is a heavenly coin, abundantly sufficient for food and raiment during a whole eternity. The reward ought to correspond with the labour; but the toil of those labouring in the vine yard of Christ must not be estimated by the work alone; for we should all say with the Apostle: " I reckon that the sufferings of this time are not worthy to be compared with the glory to come, that shall be revealed in us;" but we must estimate the labour from the grace of God dwelling in the hearts of the just, which is a " fountain of living water; springing up into eternal life. And likewise from the virtue of charity, which is infused into us by the Holy Spirit that is given to us; but a crown of eternal life is prepared by God for them that love Him, as St. James writes.

Likewise, from our union with Christ, who being the true vine, gives the greatest value to the fruit of living branches, and to the works of living members of His mystical body, of whom He is the head, and to whom He hath said: ***"Be glad and rejoice, for your reward is very great in heaven."*** In fine, will not our Lord say at the last day, when the reward will be given to those that labour in the vineyard: ***"Come, ye blessed of my Father, possess you the kingdom prepared for you from the foundation of the world: For I was hungry, and ye gave me to eat?" &c. Thus, works of charity especially relate to the labour by which we toil in the vineyard of the Lord.***

Behold, then, how precious this "penny" is, which is called by our Lord Himself a kingdom! Nor without reason is it called so, since it represents Christ no less than the treasure or pearl does. For on the coin is impressed the image of a prince, and words are inscribed on it, and the figure is round. Now, Christ is " the image of the invisible God," and the " Word" of the eternal Father, " having neither beginning of days nor end of life," which is signified by the round figure. And in fine, " All things obey money/ as Solomon saith: now, Christ is the " Lord of all," as St. Peter testifieth in the Acts of the Apostles. Wherefore, the penny" given to those labouring in the vineyard is Christ, true God, and by Him eternal life, according to St. John in his First Epistle: " And He hath given us understanding, that we may know the true God,

and may be in his true Son. This is the true God, and life eternal." (chap, v.)

But let us consider to whom this precious reward is given, which, when once possessed, we shall no more stand in need of any thing else. " Call the labourers, and pay them their hire," saith the Lord. The reward, therefore, will be given to those who labour without intermission, without negligence.

But it will not be given to those standing in the market-place, idle, or engaged in fowling, hunting, or gambling: the reward will be bestowed on the deserving, not given gratis, and much less will it be given to the undeserving. When the Apostle saith, *" The wages of sin is death; but the grace of God life everlasting,"* he therefore speaks, because, without the preventing grace of God, no one can do good so as to merit the reward of eternal life; but when grace is received, which is given "gratis," and not from our works, then the reward of good works will be eternal life.

Thus St. Augustine speaks in his Epistle to Sixtus, a priest at Rome: *"As death is the merited reward as it were of sin, so eternal life is the reward of virtue."* *(Epist. 105)* But because the same reward is given to all, we must not suppose that, in the kingdom of heaven, all the rewards are alike. The coin signifies eternal life, whether God or Christ; now eternal life, that is, God and Christ, are common to all the saints. But, as the same sun is seen more clearly by the eagle than by other birds, and as the same fire gives more warmth to those that are near it than to those at a distance, so in eternal life one will see and enjoy God more clearly and sweetly than another; for, since there is a diversity of merit, so also will there be a diversity of reward.

This may have been the reason why our Lord changed the order in the distribution of his payments, saying, *"Call the labourers, and pay them their hire, beginning from the last even to the first. So shall the last be first, and the first last. For many are called, but few chosen"* But these words relate to the grace of the New Testament, informing us that we are more happy than our fathers under the Old law, and therefore we should be grateful to God, and labour with more cheerfulness and diligence in his vineyard. The holy men that cultivated the vineyard of our Lord before the Ascension of Christ such as Adam, Noah, Abraham, Moses, and other patriarchs and prophets, who were called at the first, third, sixth, and ninth hour laboured not only for a long time because they lived longer, but, even after death, they were expecting their reward for many centuries, and some for many thousands of years.

The apostles, martyrs, and other labourers, who came to cultivate the vineyard at the eleventh hour, that is, at the last hour, according to the interpretation of St. John, laboured but for a few years, and immediately after death, having entered the kingdom of heaven, they received their reward. How great is this grace, by which, if a Christian wish, after enduring but very short labours, he can immediately ascend to that place, for which the most holy patriarchs and prophets sighed for so long a period! Not without cause did these ancient saints murmur as it were [1] when they said: *" These last have worked but one hour, and thou hast made them equal to us that have borne the burden of the day and the heats."*

But our Lord answered for us: *"Friend, I do thee no wrong: didst thou not agree with me for a penny? Take what is thine, and go thy way: I will also give to this last, even as to thee."* This answer does not mean that men under the new law receive by grace, and not by their justice, a reward equal to those under the Old law; but that they received a more abundant grace, by which they have no less laboured in the vineyard for a short time than the others did during a long period, and therefore they have justly received an equal, and even greater reward.

The Apostles certainly laboured for a short time: but they brought forth the greatest fruit in the vineyard of the Lord. When did the patriarchs or prophets, having abandoned all temporal things, ever traverse almost the whole earth, and bring so many kingdoms of the Gentiles to the true worship of God? When, in those ancient times, did so numerous an army of martyrs endure every torment and the most cruel deaths for the true faith?

When, in the Old Testament, were so many choirs of holy virgins found, who followed the spotless Lamb, and vowed and gave unto God their soul and body? Where were then so many pastors and doctors, who, watching over their flocks, fought against the wolves, that is, against heretics and pagans, by their most learned writings? Where, in fine, was so great a number of hermits and monks, and other religious men, who, emulating the life of angels, spent the day and night in the praise of God alone and in prayer?

These and other examples of the most eminent virtue belong to the New Testament and its blessings, on account of which our Lord justly concludes the parable in these words: *" Thus the last shall be first, and the first last. For many are called, but few are chosen;"* that is, many have been called to cultivate the vineyard in all ages of the world, but few have been chosen to the grace of the New Testament, by which they have produced great fruit, and have in a short time received the greatest rewards.

But we must not suppose that all who have been called at the eleventh hour, will receive a reward; but those only who have laboured, with their whole strength and for a short period, in the vineyard of the Lord. For many there are, who, knowing that this hour is the last, and that time is short, say not as they ought to do: *"Our life is short, therefore let us diligently labour that,*

in so short a period, we may bring forth much fruit."
But they speak as the foolish do in the Book of Wisdom:
"They have said, reasoning with themselves, but not right: The time of our life is short and tedious, and in the end of a man there is no remedy, and no man hath been known to have returned from hell.

Come, therefore, let us enjoy the good things that are present, and let us speedily use the creatures as in youth. Let us fill ourselves with costly wine and ointments; and let not the flower of the time pass by us. Let us crown ourselves with roses, before they be withered: let no meadow escape our riot: let us everywhere leave tokens of joy, for this is our portion, and this our lot." (chap, ii.) Such is the language of those, who either know not God, or, acknowledging Him, deny Him by their works. And these are indeed so numerous, that to them may be referred the concluding words of the parable: "Many are called, but few are chosen"

Many are called at the last hour, but few chosen, because few so labour as to be deserving of the reward. Woe therefore to us, who, being called at the last hour, spend the greater part of it in play and sleep, whilst we ought to be so careful of every moment as not to suffer one single portion of it to pass by unprofitably; for on these moments dependeth an eternity of happiness or of misery. And doubtless, in proportion as the grace granted to Christians under the New Law is greater, so much more grievously will they be punished who receive this grace in vain.

And as the last shall be first in receiving the reward, because they laboured diligently at the last hour; so also will the last be the first in receiving punishment, who shall neglect diligently to labour at the last hour.

ON THE TALENTS.

THE fourth parable is that in which our Lord thus speaks of the reward of beatitude: *" Well done, good and faithful servant, because thou hast been faithful over a few things, I will place thee over many things: enter thou into the joy of thy Lord"* (St. Matthew, chap. xxv. 21.)

In these words two things are promised to faithful servants, the most ample power and the greatest joy: *"I will place thee over many things ;"* and what these *" many things"* are, He explains in another place where it is said: *" Blessed is that servant, whom, when his Lord shall come, he shall find so doing. Amen, I say to you, he shall place him over all his goods."* (chap, xxiv. 46.)

But what means being placed *"over all the goods"* of the Lord, except to receive power over all inferior things, and to be made a partaker of that sovereignty which God possesses over the whole universe? Who can comprehend the greatness of this power? What king or emperor upon earth can be compared with the least of the saints?

But since man cannot possess such great power without having great care and trouble, therefore our Lord adds: "Enter into the joy of thy Lord." As if he wished to say, " As I make thee a partaker of the greatest power, so also do I make thee enjoy rest and pleasure, which no cares can destroy or diminish." How great this "joy" will be, which is promised to the just in heaven, is quite inexplicable, nor shall we know it before we have experienced it. But yet, from the consideration of three words in the sentence, we may in some measure conceive how great will be the " joy." The first word is " enter;" for as it is not said, May the joy of thy Lord enter into thee, but enter thou into the joy of thy Lord, this is a proof that the joy will be greater than we can conceive.

Wherefore, we shall enter into a great sea of divine and eternal joy, which will fill us within and without, and surround us on all sides. In this abundance of joy, what room will there be for sorrow? Another word is *"into the joy,"* by which an indefinite joy concerning this or that good is not promised, but a joy absolutely pleasure itself, sweetness itself, delight itself. And doth not our whole soul dissolve as it were, being surrounded with such sweetness? But the third word, *" of thy Lord,"* greatly increases this joy; for we shall enter, not into the joy which men or angels possess, but into that which God possesses, in whom are all infinite riches.

Who can conceive what this joy of the Lord will be, but He who perfectly knoweth His own infinite goodness, and enjoys it in an infinite degree? And yet, Christian soul! what thou canst not now conceive, thou wilt experience, and taste, and eternally enjoy, if thou be a good and faithful servant. Let us now consider to whom these promises relate. They relate, without doubt, to those who have faithfully endeavoured to multiply the talents entrusted to them by God. The parable is drawn from a rich man, who went into a far country, and delivered his goods to his servants. And to one he gave five talents, and to another two, and to another one, commanding them all to multiply their talents by careful and prudent business. Various are the opinions of interpreters concerning the signification of these " talents".

Some understand by *them " blessings"* given gratis; others the Holy Scriptures; others the knowledge of external things acquired by the senses, is meant by the five talents; that the two talents signify understanding and action, and the one talent understanding alone: others, in fine, consider them to refer to natural gifts, such as genius and judgment, or to the spiritual ones of faith, hope, and charity. But all agree in this, that the multiplication of the talents consists in labouring diligently for our own salvation as well as that of others. But another explanation occurs to me, not repugnant to the others, and which altogether appears to agree with what our Lord says concerning the talents. And first, the talents are called *" the goods of the Lord ;" " He delivered to them his goods;"* then the servants are commanded to multiply the talents: *" Lord, thou didst deliver to me five talents, behold I have gained other five over and above."*

Thirdly, it is said, "He gave to every one according to his proper ability." Lastly, the talent is taken away from the wicked and slothful servant. I therefore understand by the talents the souls of faithful and pious men, entrusted to the care and fidelity of bishops. These are truly the "goods" of the Lord, which are not given to us, but only committed to our care to be multiplied. Our Lord did not say to Peter, *" Feed thy sheep," but "Feed my sheep."* Other things are our own goods, although bestowed by God, as genius, judgment, the Holy Scriptures, blessings given gratis, &c. But faithful and pious souls He calls His " goods," His vineyard, His family, His spouse: for these He came into the world, for their redemption He poured out His blood, to gain these He sent His apostles, to whom He said, "I will make you to be fishers of men."

Now faithful souls are multiplied, when bishops convert sinners by word and by example. This St. Peter did when, after our Saviour had entrusted to him one hundred and twenty Christians, saying, Feed my sheep; he converted on the day of Pentecost, by his first sermon, three thousand people, then five thousand, and afterwards many thousands. ***And St. Gregory Thaumaturgus, when made bishop of Neo- Cæsarea, found only seventeen Christians: but he so multiplied them, that when he was on the point of death only seventeen infidels were left in so large a city: this circumstance St. Gregory of Nyssa relates, in his Life of St. Gregory Thaumaturgus.***

But these talents are given to each one ***"according to his proper ability"***. For God who knoweth the strength that is, the prudence, knowledge, charity, and strength of all men, commits souls to those only who He thinks are fit to bear such a burden. And, therefore, no one ought to undertake the care of souls, and especially accept of the episcopacy, unless called by Him who gives the talents, according to the ability of each one. But if otherwise, we cannot wonder that many fall under the burden: neither will it be an excuse before God to say, that their shoulders were not equal to such a burden: He will answer, Who forced thee to bear a burden beyond thy strength? Didst thou not wish, and ask, and endeavour to obtain it? Now therefore thou shalt be cast out into the exterior darkness.

In fine, the talent given to the slothful servant is taken away from him. And if we say, that the talents are the souls of the faithful, this will perfectly agree with the parable. For he who received only one talent, that is, the care of his own soul alone, will lose it if he neglect to take proper care of it: the devil will make it his property. And as the blessed possess the liberty of the sons of

God, by which they freely remain where they wish, and do whatever they desire; so on the contrary also, the wicked lose all liberty, and their hands and feet being bound, they can neither walk where they wish, nor do whatever they desire; but they are compelled to remain where they wish not, being unable to do what they wish: this is, to lose their soul.

Wherefore this interpretation, in which by the talents faithful souls are understood, is quite consistent with the parable. But how the other opinions can be reconciled, it is no easy matter to teach: they are not, however, false on this account, or to be rejected, because it is not necessary to accommodate every explanation to the parable, as St. Chrysostom wisely remarks.[1] We shall still continue our exposition, not rejecting, as we have said, the exposition of others.

Wherefore, our Lord has committed his talents to three sorts of men; to those who are perfect, such as bishops ought to be, He has given five talents, that is, a great number of people to take care of; to others less perfect, such as priests generally are, He has given two talents, that is, the fewer souls which are contained in a parish: but to others more rude and infirm, such as the common people, to each of them He has given one, that is, the care of his own soul.

These also ought, as far as they can, by words of private exhortation and good example, to lead others from sin to the path of virtue, and in this way multiply the talent entrusted to them. And what is said of bishops and priests, ought also to be understood as relating to princes and magistrates, and fathers of families. Thus writes St. Augustine: ***"Every head of a family should be by his name, the paternal love of his family. For the sake of Christ and of eternal life, he should admonish, instruct, exhort, and connect all his dependants: he should manifest love to them, and likewise exercise discipline: thus in his own house he will*** *fulfil in a certain degree, the spiritual office of a bishop." (Tractatus 51, in Johan.)*

In this sense, Constantino the Great used to say, that he was a bishop out of the church, because he was solicitous that the church should be protected and extended: but yet, he did not usurp the ecclesiastical office.

But lest any one should suppose that one man alone, or one class of men only is comprehended in this parable, because he alone who received the one talent was punished, we must know, that our Lord wishes us to understand the dangers to which superiors are exposed. For as at the last day he will reward those who do corporal works of mercy, and punish those who do them not; from which we know that greater will be the rewards of those who perform spiritual works of mercy, especially of the holy apostles and martyrs, and virgins of heroic virtue; and on the other hand, that greater will be the punishment of thieves, robbers, perjurers, and the sacrilegious, than those who give not alms to the poor: so also in this passage, because he who received the one talent which he might easily have multiplied, and yet did not, was most grievously punished, we must understand, that in proportion as bishops, pastors, and princes fail in this point, so will they be punished the more grievously, as the loss of many souls is greater than that of one.

Let us hear what St. Augustine says on the danger of the ecclesiastical state: *"Above all things, I beseech you piously and diligently to reflect, that in this life and especially at this time, nothing is more easy, pleasing, and acceptable to men, than the office of a bishop, priest, or deacon, if it be discharged in a careless or fawning manner; but before God nothing is more afflicting and offensive. Again, nothing in this life and especially at this time, is more difficult, laborious, and dangerous, than the office of a bishop, priest, or deacon; but before God nothing is more blessed, if it be fulfilled in the manner our great king commands." Epist. 147. ad Valerium.*

In the remaining part of this epistle he treats the subject in such a manner that I wish all ecclesiastics would attentively read it, and especially those who rashly aspire to the episcopacy or priesthood. For many when they have obtained what they asked for, and found what they sought after, either desert their flock, or being intent on other things, care little about attending to their flock and increasing the number of faithful and pious souls.

On the night of the birth of our Saviour, the shepherds were keeping watch over their flocks: and if this was done for senseless sheep, by those who were a figure of the shepherds of the church, how much more ought it to be done by the shepherds of that flock, for which our Saviour when on earth, watched whole nights in prayer, not for Himself certainly, but for His sheep? And if the patriarch Jacob laboured so much for the flocks of his father-in- law, Laban, that he should say, *"Day and night was I parched with heat, and with frost, and sleep departed from my eyes,"* what ought the shepherd of *the flock of Christ to do, for which He shed His blood? And if the devil goeth about as a roaring lion seeking whom he may devour, is it not proper that the good shepherd should also go about, seeking whom to save?*

But it may be said, business connected with the Church often compels one to leave his flock. I admit this, when the business is important, and only a short time is spent in attending to it: otherwise great things are to be preferred before less, and the former should be performed by ourselves, the latter by others. For if business compels us to leave our flock , more important business, even dreadful wars, compel us not to leave our flock defenceless. The trumpet of St. Paul sounds forth: *"Our wrestling is not against flesh and blood, but against principalities and powers, against the rulers of the world of this darkness, against the spirits of wickedness in the high places. (Ephesians vi. 12.)*

And if the general be absent, who shall teach the soldiers to extinguish the fiery darts of the most wicked one? Our Lord said to Peter, and through him to all pastors, **"Feed my sheep:"** He was silent on other things, to teach us that this duty was the chief duty. And in the consecration of a bishop it is said, Go, preach unto the people committed to thee; but on temporal matters nothing is added, that the bishop may be admonished, not to make temporal things equal to spiritual, much less to prefer the first before the latter. In fine, in the fourth council of Carthage, bishops are seriously commanded not to undertake by themselves the care of widows, minors, and strangers, but to entrust them to their archpriest or deacon; not to undertake the settling of wills, not to engage in law-suits for transitory things, not to be occupied with domestic cares; but to attend only to reading, prayer, and preaching. Wherefore this council, composed of two hundred and fourteen bishops, at which St. Augustine was also present, wished that bishops should commit all temporal matters to others, that they might more freely attend to the care and increase of their flock.

As this parable therefore shows us, that eternal happiness is an object especially to be desired, since it contains the highest power united with the greatest delight; so also it proves, that the means of arriving at this happiness, consists in labouring assiduously for the salvation of our own soul, and in seeking and procuring that of others. And they who refuse to endure this labour, are deprived not only of this happiness and pleasure, but are condemned to eternal torments in hell, for thus our Lord speaks **"The unprofitable servant cast ye out** *into the exterior darkness. There shall be weeping and gnashing of teeth."*

Here we should particularly notice, that the servant who is so severely punished, is not said to be wicked or impious, but only " unprofitable. " Thus although a bishop, or priest, a prince, or magistrate, or head of a family, were free from other crimes, yet should he be unprofitable, that is, neglectful of his salvation and that of his subjects, he will be cast out into "the exterior darkness, & c".

But if the unprofitable servant shall suffer this punishment, what will be done to the covetous, proud, luxurious servant, addicted to various vices? If the unprofitable servant be condemned, what an account will the impious prevaricator have to give to God, of the talents entrusted to him? Truly they that consider these things, will not seek after high places; and if they should be compelled to receive them, they will ever watch with fear and trembling, as having to give a most strict account of the souls entrusted to them.

THE PARABLE OF THE SUPPER.

THE fifth parable, which is found in St. Luke, makes the happiness of the saints like to a great supper: and truly, not without reason. For in a nuptial or royal supper, every thing is found that can delight the human sense, and exhibit the power, riches, and glory of this world. Wherefore , when king Assuerus ruled over a hundred and twenty-seven provinces, and wished to display the riches of the glory of his kingdom, and the greatness of his power, he found nothing more adapted for his purpose, than to prepare a most magnificent banquet. First, in a great banquet the eyes are delighted with the costly ornaments of the palace, with the numerous servants clad in beautiful and precious robes, with the gold and silver vases in which the viands are carried; the ears are delighted with various musical instruments, and the songs of many voices; the sense of smell is delighted with the odour of flowers, precious ointment, and scented water, & c.; the sense of taste with viands of every description, and precious wines from every land; in fine; the sense of touch is charmed by the softest and most elegant couches.

Wherefore, as in a royal or nuptial banquet, nearly every corporal good is found that can be procured on earth, not without reason did Our Lord, wishing to represent that "happiness" which in itself includes all good things, compare it to a great supper: of this we read in the Apocalypse: "Blessed are they who are called to the nuptial supper of the Lamb." We may learn how great the supper of the Lord will be, from this circumstance, that the beauty of all the glorified bodies will be, the table on which the last service is placed. But so great is the sweetness of the last course, that when St. Peter once saw the body of the Lord resplendent as the sun, he said, "It is good for us to be here." And if these things be such, what will the supper itself be, which consists in the enjoyment of the divinity!

In fine, all the good things of this world are nothing else than the rind and shell as it were, of the fruits of paradise. And if these "parings" be such, that men are enchanted with a love and desire for them, what will the fruit itself of paradise be! And if the fruit be such, what will the more solid and excellent food be! Truly it will be such, as always to be eaten without satiety, always to be desired. But we must not suppose, that the supper in heaven will be such as great princes give here on earth at their espousals; in heaven we shall be as the angels of God; ***"we shall neither marry, nor be married"*** nor shall we stand in need of food to support life. The supper therefore will consist of spiritual riches, and delights, and glory, and ornament, suitable to the state of the blessed.

Riches and delights are mentioned in this life, because we see not things more excellent. But from these we may learn, that the spiritual supper will be so superior to our most splendid banquets, as heaven is to earth, and as God who will prepare it, is above all mortals in power and majesty.

But some one will say, Why is the happiness of the

saints compared to a supper, rather than to a dinner? The reason is this; because dinner is taken at mid-day and after it business is attended to till evening: but supper is taken towards evening, when all business is finished, and afterwards come rest and sleep. Wherefore in another parable which is found in St. Matthew, respecting the Incarnation of our Lord, dinner is introduced on account of the marriage which the king made for his son. The reason is, because our Lord's Incarnation, and the marriage with His spouse the Church, were commenced at mid-day, that is, a long while before the end of the world.

After dinner, the redemption of the world, and the reconciliation of man with God, were celebrated. But when the bride shall be conducted to the palace of the bridegroom, and to the nuptial supper, all business will cease, and the sweetest sleep shall follow, that is, there will be eternal rest. This therefore is the reason, why the perfect glory of the blessed is compared to a supper, rather than to a dinner.

But it will be useful to consider what we must do, in order to be admitted to the supper. This our Lord plainly teaches us in the parable, for He saith: ***"A certain man made a great supper and invited many And they began all at once to make excuse. The first said to him: I have bought a farm, and I must needs go out and see it: I pray thee, hold me excused. And another said: I have bought five yoke of oxen, and I go to try them: I pray thee hold me excused. And another said: I have married a wife, and therefore I cannot come"*** (St. Luke xiv.)

How wonderful! Men are invited by God to the nuptial supper, and they refuse! What would they do if they were called to military service, or to undertake a long and dangerous journey? Such is the blindness of men, that they can scarcely be induced to believe what they do not see. But what is that which mortals prefer before the nuptial supper, that is, before their greatest, eternal good? Our Lord mentions three impediments to salvation, which of their own nature are not evil; but yet, too great an affection for them hinders our eternal salvation. To buy a farm, to try oxen, to marry a wife, are not sinful: but to prefer them before the kingdom of heaven, is an incredible blindness.

And yet, there are many Christians who pursue temporal goods with such ardour; and honours, dignity, and power, signified in the purchase of the farm; and riches, signified by the oxen; and pleasure, by the marriage; that they spend days and nights in seeking and enjoying them, entirely forgetting those eternal rewards which God hath promised to them that love Him. And many are not content with purchasing farms, trying yokes of oxen, and marrying; but in order as it were, more completely to neglect their salvation, they seize the farms of other men steal their oxen, and support concubines: nor do they ever consider what a misfortune it will be, for such husks of swine to be deprived of the supper of the Lord. Truly, if our Lord had promised to us worms of the earth, not a supper of infinite sweetness, but crumbs falling from that table; even then it would be advantageous for us to despise all temporal goods, that so we might possess those crumbs. What madness therefore is it, to prefer insignificant and fleeting pleasures, before this divine supper, which abounds with every eternal delight, and in which we shall sit down with the holy angels, and even with the King of Angels in heaven!

After our Lord hath shown us what are the impediments to our being present at the great supper, He also added the means by which they may be removed: He continues in the parable: " Then the master of the house being angry, said to his servant: Go out quickly into the streets and lanes of the city, and bring in hither the poor and the feeble, and the blind and the lame." Because the rich were occupied in buying farms, and oxen, and marrying, they refused to attend the supper of their great Master. He therefore calls the poor, who have neither money to purchase farms and oxen, nor are able to support their wives, if they can find any. He calls the feeble, who cannot visit farms, nor buy oxen, nor marry wives: He calls the blind, who cannot see farms, nor manage oxen nor easily find a wife: He calls the lame, who cannot without the greatest difficulty, walk to a farm, manage oxen, or dance at a marriage. These therefore being free from every impediment by which the others are bound, and being admitted to the supper, ought justly to rejoice that God made them feeble, and blind, and lame.

Many in this life complain, that they were born poor, or that they are often infirm, or blind, or lame, and they appear to be most unhappy thereat. But they know not what good things God hath prepared for them hereafter, on account of that very affliction which men call ***"misfortune:"*** but if they did know, they would certainly be glad and rejoice. No one ought to complain of the providence of God, but in all things give thanks to God the best of Fathers, who taketh care of us: to His will we should always resign ourselves.

But although we must thus act, yet in this place those are properly considered poor, who are poor in spirit, not in riches; who are infirm, not in strength, but in confidence in themselves; who are blind, not in sight, but to craftiness; who are lame, not in their feet, but in their affections. I will explain my meaning more plainly. The poor who are admitted to the supper of the Lord, are those who hearing the words of the Apostle, do not wish to become rich: and if they possess money, do not hoard it up, nor spend it in vanity, but in doing what the Holy Spirit speaks by the mouth of David: *" **He hath distributed, he hath given to the poor; his justice remaineth for ever and ever.**"*

The infirm are those who confide not in their virtue,

nor glory in their strength. The blind are they who truly believe what they do not see, especially as regards the rewards of the just, and the torments of the wicked. For he who is truly persuaded, that the rewards of the blessed are indeed most glorious and eternal, and the torments of the wicked most dreadful and everlasting, will not certainly be attached to the earth nor to its goods, but will fix his heart there, where alone is true joy. In fine, the lame are those and they can justly aspire to the supper of the Lord whose right foot is much longer than the left; that is, whose love of God and affection for eternal goods, are greater than the love of themselves and of temporal things, signified by the left foot.

But let us consider the sentence of our great Master, against those who blindly and most foolishly despised His Supper: *" **But I say unto you, that none of those men that were invited shall taste of my supper.** "* Our Lord knew well, that they who had been invited, and who through love for present goods despised the future ones as useless, would hunger after that supper with an incredible ardour when the senses of the flesh were extinct in death, and all earthly things had been removed: for the prophet David saith: *"**They shall return at evening, and shall suffer hunger like dogs; and shall go round about the city**"* (Psalm lviii.)

At evening, when the day of this present life is finished, they will return and repent, but their sorrow will be useless, and they will be hungry like mad dogs, and go round about the City of God, seeking to obtain, if they can, a few crumbs from that supper. But the sentence of the Lord is fixed *" **None of them shall taste of my supper** "O! if thou didst know, my soul, the meaning of these words, "None of them shall taste of my supper;" if thou couldst comprehend how great will be the hunger of those miserable men, and of what sweet food they will for ever be deprived!*

And what would they then give, if they could but

taste of that for which they so ardently long? But nought will they obtain, even if the whole world were at their disposal, and they were willing to renounce it. Since then this is the case, let us be converted whilst we have time, whilst it is our day, whilst penance is profitable. Let us now hunger after that most delicious supper, not as mad and unclean dogs, who think of nothing but of their food, but as men endowed with reason; let us hunger after the food of eternal life, and the bread of angels, even that hidden manna *" **which no one knoweth but he that receiveth**"* and which God Himself enjoyeth from eternity unto eternity.

And let us so live in this our exile, as not to be in love with it, but to sigh after our true country. When we shall have arrived there, we shall not be obliged to " go round about" the city, but we shall enter the open gate; and being admitted to the supper of the Lord, we shall be filled with the bread of life and the water of wisdom, a most sweet and pleasant food.

THE PARABLE OF THE WISE
AND FOOLISH VIRGINS.

THE last parable is that which makes the happiness of the saints like to a royal marriage, to which ten virgins were invited, five being wise and five foolish. We shall first briefly explain who is the bride, and who the bridegroom; then how excellent a good is signified by the word "marriage;" and lastly, what is required for our attaining so great an object.

First then, no one can doubt but that Christ is the bridegroom. This is expressed by St. John the Baptist, where speaking of Christ he says: "He that hath the bride, is the bridegroom; but the friend of the bridegroom, who standeth and heareth him, rejoiceth with joy because of the bridegroom s voice." Our Lord Himself also intimates the same in the parable of the king who made a marriage for his son. The Apostle confirms the same, in his Epistle to the Corinthians: ***" I have espoused you to one husband, that I may present you as a chaste virgin to Christ"***

So also does St. John in the Apocalypse: ***" Let us be glad and rejoice, and give glory to him; for the marriage of the Lamb is come, and his wife hath pre-***

pared herself:" and again, ***"Blessed are they that are called to the marriage supper of the Lamb."*** It is equally certain, that the Church is the bride. This the Apostle clearly asserts in his Epistle to the Ephesians: ***"Therefore as the Church is subject to Christ, so also let the wives be to their husbands in all things. Husbands, love your wives, as Christ also loved the Church, and delivered himself up for it, that he might sanctify it For this cause shall a man leave his father and mother, and shall cleave to his wife, and they shall be two in one flesh. This is a great sacrament; but I speak in Christ and in the Church."*** (chap. v. 24, &c.)

But although the Church be the spouse of Christ, and the faithful be called the Sons of the Church, because by baptism she has brought them forth, as it were, for Christ; yet, because the Church is nothing more than an assembly of the faithful, therefore all pious souls are individual spouses, as the Church is an universal spouse.

For not falsely doth the Church sing of holy virgins, ***" Come, spouse of Christ, and receive -the crown which the Lord hath prepared for thee for ever"*** But although holy virgins are, in a special manner, called spouses of Christ, because they have rejected a carnal marriage, in order to be spiritually married to Christ alone; yet other Christian souls are also " spouses" of Christ, for they are espoused to Him by faith, united to Him by charity, and aspire to a consummation of the spiritual marriage in the kingdom of heaven.

But if we could sufficiently conceive what a good it will be for the human soul to be united with marriage in Christ, we should find nothing more honourable, nothing more useful, nothing more sweet, either in this world or in the next. Great is the glory, advantage, and sweetness in serving the King of kings; greater to be numbered amongst his friends and domestics; the greatest to be called a son of God and the brother of Christ.

But to become the *" spouse"* of God, a partner of His throne, of His crown, and of all His titles, appears to me to be more than the greatest, if I may so speak. This it is of which our Lord speaks in Isaias concerning spiritual eunuchs: "I will give to them in my house, and within my walls, a name better than sons and daughters ;" that is, I will give to them the name of a spouse. Who can comprehend, how noble, how honourable and sweet it will be, not only to behold God and to converse with him, but to become one spirit with Him, and to be transformed into Him? These are the words of the Apostle: " He who is joined to a harlot, is made one body

But he who is joined to the Lord, is one spirit :" and again, "But we all beholding the glory of the Lord with open face, are transformed into the same image from glory to glory, as by the Spirit of the Lord" (2 Epist. to the Corinth, iii. 18.) How great will be the pleasure, when being united to God and irradiated by the brightness of His countenance, we shall be transformed into His brightness, and made most like unto Him! "We shall be like to him" saith St. John, " because we shall see him as he is." We shall be like to Him, not only as images created according to His likeness; but like in glory, in beatitude, in happiness.

St. Paul the apostle, in that wonderful rapture he had when he was caught up into paradise; heard secret words which it was not in the power of man to utter; and yet he was so absorbed in God, that he knew not whether he was in the body or out of the body. How great, therefore, will be that most happy union of the soul with God, when absorbed and immersed in the sea of His sweetness, she will be "one spirit" with God! So great will be the joy, that as St. Bernard says, *" All other joy compared with it will be sorrow all sweetness will be bitterness; all honour, dishonour; whatever else, in fine, can delight us, will be troublesome."* (Epistle 114).

But since this union of the most beautiful spouse with a blessed soul be ineffable, let us rather inquire from the present parable what are the conditions on which we can be admitted to this most happy marriage? These we shall learn from the qualities of the wise virgins, for they alone entered into the nuptials of the heavenly spouse. The qualities or conditions are five; first, that we be virgins; secondly, that we be prudent; thirdly, that we have our lamp lighted; fourthly, that we have oil in it; and lastly, that we watch, and by watching diligently await the coming of the bridegroom.

As far as regards the first condition, the spouses of Christ ought all to be virgins, not necessarily in the flesh, but in faith and morals, as St. Augustine justly explains in his Sermon on these words of the Apostle: "I have espoused you to one husband, that I may present you as a chaste virgin to Christ." By a chaste virgin he understands the whole Church of Corinth, in which it is evident that all were not virgins in the flesh, since the Apostle in his First Epistle admonishes married people of their duties. In this parable, therefore, all those are virgins who are not corrupted in their faith and morals, and who, declining from evil, do not defile their souls.

But, because it is not sufficient for perfect justice to decline from evil, but also to do good, therefore the second condition is added, that we be prudent, not foolish. Nor must we think it sufficient, if we injure no one, nor kill any one, nor steal, nor bear false testimony; but we must consider our last end, and adopt the means to attain it. And because this end is eternal life, and the means the merit of good works, therefore the third condition is added, that our lamp be lighted, which signifies good works. This St. Augustine teaches in the above-mentioned place, and our Lord Himself, where He says: "So let your light shine before men, that they may see your good works, and glorify your leather who is in heaven"

But since good works spring from charity as from a root, and cannot be preserved unless nourished by the same charity, as a lamp necessarily goes out if oil be wanting; therefore, a fourth condition is required, that the prudent virgin always have oil in her lamp.

St. Augustine teaches that charity is signified by oil, because, as oil is superior to all liquids, so charity is superior to all virtues, according to the Apostle: "And I show unto you yet a more excellent way;" and again: "And now there remain faith, hope, charity, these three; but the greater of these is charity. If, therefore, we should prefer anything in our heart, or make it equal with charity, immediately she departs; for she ought either to have the first place, and reign in our heart, or she will leave us. And because oil is a most subtle liquid, which easily ascends above other things, the power of the oil of charity is so great in ascending, that if it be poured out on the soul of a public sinner, immediately it draws that soul up, and of a sinner makes a saint, of a carnal man makes a spiritual man.

I will even venture to say, that if this oil were poured on the souls of the damned, or could drop on the devils themselves, we should immediately behold them all ascend on high. And if, on the contrary, this oil were to desert the souls of the holy angels, apostles, martyrs, and virgins, they would quickly descend down into hell.

Behold, then, the excellence of this oil, and how justly those virgins are called foolish who have not this oil. But there is also another reason why charity is signified by oil, because it maketh things that are hard and rough soft and pliable. This oil renders the yoke sweet, of which our Lord speaks, ***"My yoke is sweet." What made the yoke of obedience sweet to the Apostles, of going into the whole world and preaching the Gospel to every creature, but the oil of charity? What made*** *the yoke of patience sweet to the martyrs, to endure so great and unheard of torments, but the oil of charity? What made the yoke of poverty, of chastity, and of obedience, so sweet to many thousands of religious men and women, but the yoke of charity?*

Nothing is more sweet to a lover than to show his love for his Beloved by doing or enduring great and difficult things for his sake. There now remaineth a fifth condition, which is the most important of all, being especially commanded by our Lord in this parable, viz., watchfulness: ***"Watch ye therefore, because you know not the day nor the hour."***

And in order that these words may be deeply impressed upon the hearts of the faithful, He constantly repeats Watch;" and again, in St. Matthew: ***"Wherefore, be you also ready, because at what hour you know not the Son of man will come ;" and in St. Mark: " Watch ye therefore, for you know not when the Lord of the house cometh: at even, or at midnight, or at the cock crowing, or in the morning; lest coming on a sudden, he find you sleeping. And what I say to you I say to all: Watch." And in St. Luke: " Blessed are those servants whom the Lord when he cometh shall find watching." And by the apostle Peter He speaketh: " Be prudent therefore, and watch in prayer ;" and by St. Paul also: Therefore let us not sleep, as others do; but let us watch and be sober;" and by St. John: "Behold I come as a thief: blessed is he that watcheth."***

All these passages signify, that the coming of the Lord to judgment, whether at the end of the world, or at each one's death in particular, is uncertain; and therefore God requires of us that we should always watch, waiting in expectation of His coming, that so He may find us prepared, and may not be compelled to exclude us, with the foolish virgins, from the marriage feast. Wherefore, to ***" sleep" meaneth nothing more than to be careless*** *of death and judgment, or so to live as never to care or think of so important a matter, on which dependeth eternal salvation. But corporal sleep is not forbidden the faithful, otherwise it would not be said in the parable, "They all slumbered and slept:"only forgetfulness and want of consideration are forbidden.*

Every Christian therefore, to whom the salvation of his soul is dear, ought everyday, morning and evening, shutting the door of his heart against all other business, attentively consider that this day or night may possibly be his last: and therefore he should seriously watch, lest he be found unprepared. All men dislike the thought of death, and gladly turn their mind to the consideration of something else; but the sick man dislikes the bitter physic, and yet through love of life he willingly takes it.

So also it behoves a prudent man to esteem the loss of his soul more than the fear of death; and therefore, again and again, he should think that there is no hour in which he may not die. For when this thought deeply descends into the bottom of our heart, it will soon change the whole and from, carnal make him spiritual, from a sinner a saint: so that he will no more fear, but love the coming of the Lord. Not without reason, then, does our Lord so frequently exhort us to watch, nor Ecclesiasticus to admonish us: *" In all thy works remember thy last end, and thou shalt never sin." (chap, vii.)* For who, remembering that he is hastening to judgment, and that quickly he will have to stand before the divine tribunal, can dare to sin before his Judge? We are all hastening every moment to judgment; but yet, so great is human blindness, that even on the journey itself we offend our Judge, and most justly provoke His anger against us.

Who is there, when condemned to suffer death, and being led out to execution, would laugh and joke, and speak of his former crimes, or of attaining dignities, and gaining money by traffic, unless he were mad? Now, we are all certainly condemned to death, nor can any son of Adam escape the sentence: our mortal life is nothing but a journey towards death: but yet, on this journey, which cannot be a long one, how do the generality of Christians act? What do they think of, what do they speak of, what are they busy about, but honours, riches, pleasures, and even wickedness, as if they would never die! And what is this but to sleep over serious things, and to watch over foolish things?

Justly, then, doth our Lord cry out: " ***Watch, watch;***" blessed are those who, excited by these words, reflect where they are, and whither they are going, and so endeavour to have their lamp burning and filled with oil, that when the cry shall be heard, " Behold the spouse cometh, go ye forth to meet him" they may with joy run forth to meet the Bridegroom, and enter with him into the marriage. But woe to them who, forgetful of this, and deaf to the voice of God, shall be found sleeping with their lamps extinguished: being excluded from the delights of the marriage-feast, they will in vain exclaim, "Lord, Lord, open unto us"

ON THE PRIZE.

HAVING explained a few of the parables which are to be found in the gospel, there now only remains the explanation of those names which are used in St. Paul's First Epistle to the Corinthians; these are the "Prize" and "Crown." Of the former the Apostle thus speaks: *" Know you not that they that run in the race, all run indeed, but one receiveth the prize; so run that you may obtain." (chap. ix. 24.)*

The same Apostle in his Epistle to the Corinthians teaches, that by the "prize" eternal happiness is signified; he says, *"But one thing I do, forgetting the things that are behind, and stretching forth myself to those that are before, I press towards the mark, to the prize of the supernal vocation of God in Christ Je-sus"* (chap. iii. 13, 14.) Wherefore the prize is in heaven, and to it the Almighty invites us by His Son Christ Jesus. The prize which the kings of this world offer us, is no very valuable object; but our " heavenly prize" is in every way most glorious, whether we consider God who promises it, a Prince of infinite power and glory, of whom the prophet sings, *"Thy magnificence is ele-*

vated above the heavens ;" or whether we remember, that the combatants are His children and the brothers of Christ, whom the King their Father, would not certainly invite to run in the race, unless the prize was so great that it might justly be desired, even by the sons of God.

But it is more important for us to know, what is the meaning of running for the prize, and by what art we may so run as to be able to gain it. To run for the prize means nothing more, than faithfully to observe all the commandments of the Lord our God. That the " race" signifies the law of the Lord, David testifies where he says, *"Blessed are the undefiled in the way, who walk in the law of the Lord I have run the way of thy commandments, when thou didst enlarge my heart."* (Psalm cxviii.)

Wherefore, they who run "the way" of the commandments, run in the race for the prize. Now the art of so running that we may gain the prize, includes three points: First, we must not go out of the course, for they who do so, however quickly they may run, will never reach the goal, because they run not for the prize, but at an uncertainty. This the Apostle tells us he carefully avoided; " I therefore so run, not as at an uncertainty." What is it to run out of the race, except not to run in the way of the commandments, and to turn aside to the right or to the left?

For example: the law says, *" Thou shalt love thy neighbour as thyself;"* he that does this, runs in the race and for the prize. But he who loves his neighbour with so great a love as not to fear offending God for his sake, he turns aside to the right and runs out of the race; he runs not for the prize, but at an uncertainty. And the more benefits he bestows upon that individual who becomes an "idol" to him, the more does he wander, and the farther does he depart from the prize. But on the other hand, he that loves not his neighbour as much as he ought to do, and when he sees him in want, and " shuts up his bowels from him," as St. John expresses it, then he turns aside to the left, and neither runs in the race nor for the prize, even though he should appear to perform many good works. We must, therefore, love our neighbours as ourselves, neither more nor less; that is, we ought so to act towards our neighbour, as to do to him, what we should wish to be done to ourselves.

This is the explanation given by Christ our teacher, who gave the commandment. What I have said concerning the love of our neighbour, which is the positive command, may also be said of the negative commands. For he that steals, declines to the right of the commandment, *" Thou shalt not steal"* and thus turns aside from the course; he however that steals not, but squanders away his own substance, declines to the left, and in like manner turns aside from the course. But the just man, who alone remains in the course, would no less depart from it if he stole, than if he squandered his goods, because liberality, which relates to justice, has two opposite vices, avarice and prodigality. The conclusion is, that he who wishes to remain in the race, must be entirely free from mortal sin.

The second condition is, that he who wishes to gain the prize, must run quickly and with perseverance. He runs quickly, who observes the "commandments" with a fervent will, according to the words of the Psalmist, *"Blessed is the man that feareth the Lord, in His commands he delights exceedingly;" and the Apostle says, "Fervent in spirit serving the Lord."* He runs with perseverance, who is never fatigued nor ceases running, knowing what is written, *"He only that perseveres to the end shall be saved"*

But to run quickly, not to be fatigued, nor to interrupt our course these seem almost contrary to one another, or at least very difficult; for he that runs quickly, is soon fatigued and ceases running; whilst he that wishes not to be tired, goes slowly and perseveres on his course at a moderate pace. These remarks are true, and therefore few arrive at the prize. It is, however, absolutely necessary for him that wishes to gain the prize, to run both quickly and with perseverance, because the time is short and the way is long.

But if Christians wish to imitate those that run for a corruptible crown, they can easily run quickly and without intermission for ***"an incorruptible crown."*** What do those do who contend for the corruptible prize? They carry nothing burthensome, they cast off their garments, that so they may run free and unencumbered. This, therefore, should Christians do; they should cast off the burthens of worldly cares, and the garments of carnal desires, or at least every inordinate affection to earthly goods. And when this is done, they must glory not in their own strength, but place all their hope in God; then they will not be fatigued by running quickly in the race. This is not my doctrine, but that of Isaias and St. Paul; the former thus speaks: ***"But they that hope in the Lord shall renew their strength They shall run and not be weary, they shall walk and not faint."*** (chap. xl. 31.)

And the Apostle writes: ***" This therefore I say brethren, the time is short; it remaineth, that they also who have wives, be as if they had none. And they that weep, as though they wept not; and they that rejoice, as if they rejoiced not; and they that buy, as though they possessed not. And they that used this world, as if they used it not; for the fashion of this world passeth away."*** (1 Epist. to Corinth, vii. 29, & c.)

By these words, the Apostle does not forbid Christians from marrying, nor from weeping in adversity, nor rejoicing in prosperity, nor purchasing necessary things, or using the goods of this world; but he admonishes us, in all these things to use that moderation, and to be as little attached to them, as if they did not belong to us.

The devout Melania is an example for us in this respect; she was a noble Roman lady, of whom St. Jerome thus speaks in his Epitaph on Blosilla: *" **St.. Melania is a pattern of true nobility among the Christians of our time; for whilst the corpse of her husband was still warm, not yet being buried, she lost her two sons together. I am about to relate a thing almost incredible, but Christ is my witness it is not false. Who would not suppose that she would tear her hair, her garments, and strike her breast, like one mad? but not one tear did she shed, she stood unmoved, and throwing herself at the feet of Christ, as if she actually embraced Him, she smiled saying, "More freely shall I now serve thee, Lord, because thou hast delivered me from so great a burthen"***

Thus St. Jerome, who by this example shows us who those are that have wives, and children, and other goods of this world, as if they had them not, in order that they might run for the prize more freely. But we have a still more moving example in holy Job, who in one day lost all his sons and daughters, as well as his whole substance; and thus he lay full of ulcers on a dunghill, who a little while before, was esteemed most happy among all the Orientals. And yet, as if all these misfortunes did not concern him, he uttered these words so full of wisdom: ***"Naked came I out of my mother's womb, and naked shall I return thither; the Lord gave and the Lord hath taken away; as it hath pleased the Lord, so is it done; blessed be the name of the Lord."*** (chap. i. 21.) In fine, St. Peter and the other Apostles who first followed Christ in running for the prize, that they might teach us what is required in the same race, thus speak: ***"Behold we have left all things, and have followed thee; what therefore shall we have ?"***

Our Lord approving what they had done, thus answers, clearly promising them the prize: ***"Amen, I say to you, that you who have followed me, in the regeneration, when the Son of man shall sit on the seat of*** *his majesty, you also shall sit on twelve seats, judging the twelve tribes of Israel."* (St. Matthew xix. 28.)

The third condition is, that he who wishes for the prize, must be united with Christ. For as the Apostle saith, ***"All run indeed, but one receiveth the prize;" now this "one" is doubtless our Saviour, who " hath rejoiced as a giant to run the way ;"*** and of Him St. John speaks: ***" And no man hath ascended into heaven, but he that descended from heaven, the Son of man who is in heaven."*** (chap. iii. 13.) But Christ hath not ascended alone, but with all those who were " one" with Him; that is, who were true and living members of His body, of which He is the head. Wherefore all who run labour in vain, even though they should give all their goods to the poor, and deliver their body to be burned, unless they are joined to Christ by faith and charity, and become one with Him, as He says in St. John, ***" That they may be one, as we also are one, I in them, and thou in me, that they may be made perfect in one. "*** (chap, xvii. 22.)

But there is also another way of being united with Christ, which in a wonderful manner helps us to run quickly and with perseverance. Christ as man ran for the prize, although as God He is the "prize" itself; He is ***" true God and life eternal,"*** as St. John testifies; and this also our Saviour himself tells us, ***" I am the way, and the truth, and the life"***.

As the truth, He guides us; as the way, He leads us after Him; as the life, He brings us to Himself. In order to obtain the prize then, nothing is more useful than, for us never to turn away our eyes from Him, but to exclaim with the prophet: " My eyes are ever towards the Lord" He that keeps the eye of his soul united with his prize, neither sees nor hears what his neighbours say or do, whether they smile or mock at him; he heeds not the opinions of others, whether they praise or dispraise him;

but he says with David, **_"And I became as a man that heareth not,"_** and with the Apostle, **_"But to me it is a very small thing to be judged by you, or by man's day."_** (1 Cor iv.3)

The nearer he approaches the prize, the more does he see the greatness of it; and this greatness gives him additional strength, and induces him though wearied and fainting, not to interrupt his course. Wherefore, whoever aspires after this heavenly prize, must not turn aside from the course of the divine commands, he must run quickly and with perseverance; and being joined to Christ with true faith and charity, he must never turn away his eyes from the prize.

ON THE CROWN.

THE last name given to eternal happiness, is " a crown of justice" of which St. Paul thus speaks in the same chapter that he mentions the prize: " And every one that striveth for the mastery, refraineth himself from all things: and they indeed that they may receive a corruptible crown; but we an incorruptible one." (1 Corinth, ix. 25.) In this passage by the word " mastery" is not meant the race in the course, but rather a contest or battle; and that this comparison is different from the former, the words following prove: " I therefore so run, not as at an uncertainty: I so fight, not as one beating the air:" and so also do these words addressed to Timothy: "I have fought a good fight, I have finished my course, I have kept my faith. As to the rest, there is laid up for me a crown of justice;" & c. (2 to Timothy, iv. 7.)

In both these passage St. Paul distinguishes the course from the fight; and in one of the comparisons he uses the word " prize," and in the other the word " crown," which names are evidently distinct.

Now by the "crown" is meant eternal happiness, and this is called by St. Paul " a crown of justice," because it is given as a reward for good works. In St. James's Epistle it is called "the crown of life," because it comprehends life eternal.

By St. Peter it is named "a never-fading crown of glory." In fine, the prophet Isaias says: "In that day the Lord of hosts shall be a crown of glory, and a garland of joy to the residue of his people, "(xxviii. 5.) From this passage we may conclude, that the crown of which St. Paul speaks, and which is given to the victorious in battle, is a prize most high and noble, since God Himself will be the crown encircling and adorning the heads of the residue of His people that is, of those few among His people who shall gain the victory, by having been valiant in war. And as ***"many are called, but few are chosen"*** a truth evident from the testimony of Scripture; so the crown of the Saints will be the more glorious in the day of judgment, because so few will obtain it.

Let us now consider what is the nature of the contest we are engaged in, and what we must do to gain the victory. The contest indeed is most terrible, and the struggle most dangerous, especially if it be compared with that contest in which men on earth engage, for a corruptible crown. The Apostle alludes to the games of the circus, which took place in the presence of the people. But the combatants fought with men like themselves, and used the same weapons, and were equally exposed to the danger of popular derision or ignominy. But Christians have to fight with enemies whom they see not, and by whom they themselves are observed: they are most numerous, strong, and crafty; their arms are not alike; the contest is carried on before God and his angels, and for a crown of life eternal, and at the risk of incurring -everlasting death: in fine, the contest is not easy or imaginary, but real and most dreadful.

Our antagonists are demons, whom the Scripture at one time names lions and at another, dragons and basilisks. And we also have traitors in our own houses that is, in our bodies, the concupiscence of the flesh which wars against the spirit, as St. Peter saith: ***"Dearly beloved, I beseech you as strangers and pilgrims, to refrain yourselves from carnal desires which war against the soul"*** (1 Epist. xi.) Moreover, what is still most miserable, this contest takes place at the same time that we run in the race: and therefore the Apostle joins these two together that we may know how, whilst running for the prize, we are impeded throughout our whole course by these enemies, and hence that we must both run and fight at the same time. !

If Christians did but consider these truths and know their true condition, truly they would not so easily squander away their time in temporal trifles, in jokes, plays, and banquets; in accumulating money and seeking after honours, as if their chief happiness consisted in these things: but they would listen to the Apostle crying out to them: ***" Therefore take unto you the armour of God, that you may be able to resist in the evil day, and to stand in all things perfect. Stand therefore, having your loins girt about with truth, and having on the breast plate of justice. And in all things taking the shield of faith, wherewith you may be able to extinguish all the fiery darts of the most wicked one. And take unto you the helmet of salvation, and the sword of the Spirit, (which is the word of God.) By all prayer and supplication praying at all times in the Spirit,"*** *&c.* (Epist. to Ephesians, vi. 13, &c.) O ! what an exhortation is this; how full of terror how earnest! especially if we ponder on the words, ***" By all prayer and supplication, praying at all times."*** And yet, how many of us so act as if we neither had to run in the race, nor fight in the battle!

And now, I ask, what is to be done, that we prove

victorious in such a dreadful contest? St. Paul tells us when he says: ***"And every one that striveth for the mastery, refraineth himself from all things: and they indeed that they may receive a corruptible crown; but we an incorruptible one"***

The meaning of these words is this: those combatants, that they might obtain a corruptible crown, abstain from all those things which might weaken their body, and render them unfit to engage in such a ludicrous contest, viz., from excessive eating and drinking, from carnal delights, from domestic cares, and from all other things, however pleasant or useful, which might retard or prevent the victory. We therefore who labour for ***"an incorruptible crown,"*** ought much more to refrain from every thing that may weaken our soul, and render it unfit for that terrible fight, and for running the race in the course. And what things weaken the soul? Excessive eating, indulgence in sleep, too frequent visiting, hunting, boisterous laughter and singing; not reading good books, not praying, not meditating, not bewailing our sins, nor bringing forth worthy fruits of penance. From these ought we to abstain, if we wish our soul to be strong and fit to run in the race and fight in battle. "Take heed," saith our Saviour, ***"lest your hearts be overcharged with surfeiting and drunkenness, and the cares of this life, and that day come upon you suddenly."***

But on the other hand, the food of the soul which makes it strong, is fasting; the refreshment of the soul is prayer; the sleep of the soul holy contemplation; the purgation from noxious humours an humble confession of our sins; the joy and delight of the soul tears of compunction; and the triumph of the soul, the crucifixion of the flesh and the concupiscence thereof. ***"They that are Christs,"*** saith St. Paul, " have crucified their flesh, with the vices and concupiscences:" and again, ***"I so fight, not as one beating the air: but I chastise my*** *__body, and bring it into subjection, lest perhaps when I have preached to others, I myself should become a cast-away.__*" (1 Cor ix.26, 27) Behold the true explanation of these words, *__"Every one that striveth for the mastery, refraineth himself from all things."__* I so fight, he says, in the contest that I abstain from all those things, which can please the body and which wage war against me; these are my carnal concupiscences. But by chastising my body by fastings and watchings, and other mortifications of the flesh, I reduce it into subjection that it may not rebel against the soul, nor serve my enemies.

But who does not fear and tremble with his whole heart, when he remembers these words: "Lest perhaps when I have preached to others, I myself should become a cast-away?" If this vessel of election called by God Himself to be an Apostle, and who was rapt up into the third heaven, feared lest he should become a "cast-away," if he did not chastise his body and bring it into subjection, who amongst us will not also fear to be condemned, unless we crucify our flesh with its vices and concupiscences?

This example of the Apostle ought truly to admonish all men, that they must not venture to hope for the crown, unless they be seriously converted; unless they bring forth worthy fruits of penance, and endeavour by every possible means to bring the flesh into subjection to the spirit. But how deplorable are the blindness and foolishness of the many, who mind not these things, nor abstain from what is unlawful, but live so securely as if they had received a most assured promise from God, that their salvation was certain! But this is only another proof, as we have already said, that few are saved, and "that many are called but few are chosen."

Unto Thee then do I fly, good Lord! I am thy servant, and the son of thy hand maid: I desire with my whole soul that heavenly prize and most glorious crown, which Thou hast prepared and promised to those that love Thee. I know the greatness of the contest and the length of the course; *I know my weakness, and I confess before Thee who searchest the reins and the heart, that I possess little or no virtue: neither am I ignorant of the great power and cruel hatred of my invisible enemies, who lament that we so insignificant are destined for that immense glory, from which they fell by pride. " Enlighten my eyes that I never sleep in death ;" increase my strength, lest I faint on the way: may Thy grace defend me, " lest at any time my enemy say: "I have prevailed against him." But what I ask for myself, I ask for all my Brethren also; and especially for those placed by Thee in high dignities, whether ecclesiastical or secular: their danger is so much the -greater, as their functions are more excellent. But the more glorious will be their crown, if they perform their duties properly; and on the other hand, the more terrible the punishment if through their fault those souls perish, whom Thou hast redeemed by Thy precious blood.*

LAUS DEO SEMPER.

Notes

PREFATIO

1. *Already translated*

1. THE EXTENT OF THE KINGDOM OF GOD.

1. Especially St. Augustine and St. Thomas, the prince of scholastic writers.

2. THE INHABITANTS OF THE KINGDOM OF GOD.

1. See Alban Butler, Sept. 29th, on St. Michael.
2. These are two pure Hebrew words; the first means *" to burn, or burn up;" the second, " to be like the Most High"* [Vide Genesius Dict, in Voce, translated by Leo.]
3. See the work on the " Heavenly Hierarchy," ascribed by some to St. Dionysius the Areopagite.

4. ALL THE BLESSED ARE KINGS.

1. And a very powerful one.

5. THE HAPPINESS ENJOYED IN THE KINGDOM OF GOD.

1. I speak de facto, not de jure.
2. But I cannot mention his name.
3. Not having the passage in Greek by me, I cannot say whether this translation is correct.
4. "Et absterget Deus omnem lacrimam ab oculis eorum et mors ultra non erit neque luctus neque clamor neque dolor erit ultra quae prima abierunt "

6. WHAT IMPORTANCE MEN ATTACH TO EARTHLY KINGDOMS, AND WHAT IMPORTANCE OUGHT TO BE ATTACHED TO THE KINGDOM OF HEAVEN.

1. Which has always been considered most obligatory by every nation, even by the most cruel enemies.
2. Which you may obtain, if you wish, by the grace of God which is never wanting.
3. Father Caraffa was accustomed to say, that if men thoroughly knew the truths of eternity, and compared the goods and evils of this life with those of the next, the world would become a desert, because there would be no one that would attend to the affairs of this life. (See the "Spirit" of St. Liguori.

8. THE SECOND MEANS OF ATTAINING TO THE KINGDOM OF GOD.

1. See his epistle to Eustocliium, the daughter of Paula. It is perhaps one of the most interesting and instructive amongst his letters. He thus commences: "Si cuncta corporis mei membra verterentur in linguas, et omnes artus humanâ voce resonarent, nihil dignum Sanctæ ac venerabilis Paulæ virtutibus dicerem." His account of her leaving Toxotius and Ruffina her children, and how they endeavoured to stay her departure, is most affecting. The description of her death and burial in Jerusalem, is also truly edifying. He ends in these words: "Vale, O Paula, et cultoris tui ultimam senectutem orationibus juva. Fides et opera tua Christo te sociant: prteseiis facilius quod postulas, impetrabis. Exegi monumentum tuura aere perennius, quod nulla destruere possit yetustas. Incidi elogium Sepulchro tuo, quod huic Volumini subdidi; tit quacunque npster sermo pervenit; Te laudataui, Te in Bethelem conditam Lector agnoscat."
2. See her life in Surius.

9. THE THIRD MEANS OF ATTAINING THE KINGDOM OF GOD.

1. One would suppose.
2. And he himself.
3. As it is called.

10. THE FOURTH MEANS OF ATTAINING THE KINGDOM OF GOD.

1.   As well as many others like him.

1. ON THE BEAUTY OF THE CITY OF GOD.

1.   Not as it appears now.

2. ON THE CONCORD AND PEACE OF THE CITY OF GOD.

1.   See the Apocalypse, chap. xii This battle seems by the context, not properly to belong to the expulsion of the wicked spirits out of heaven when they sinned , but to some efforts of theirs when they were vanquished by Christ in the mystery of our Redemption.' (Alban Butler Dedication of St. Michael, Sept. 29.)

3. ON THE LIBERTY OF THE CITY OF GOD.

1.   Like the former.

4. ON THE SITUATION AND FORM OF THE CITY OF GOD.

1.   So that it is square in every part.

8. ON THE MEAT AND DRINK IN THE CITY OF GOD.

1.   That is, the wisdom by which they perfectly see God, and the charity whereby they perfectly love Him.
2.   St. Jerome also says, " Oro te, Frater charissime, inter hæc vivere, ista meditari, nihil aliud nosse, nihil quærere; nonne tibi videtur jam hie in terris Regni ecolestis habitaculum." (Epist. ad Paulinum.)

9. ON THE MYSTICAL FOUNDATION OF THE CITY OF GOD.

1. Which God forbid.

10. ON THE MYSTICAL GATE OF THE CITY OF GOD.

1. It was a saying of St. Jerome, "that the Apocalypse contained as many mysteries as it had words." It would have been well, had Newton, Faber, Bickersteth, Keith, &c., remembered these words, when they were publishing their opinions on various chapters of the Apocalypse. If St. Jerome could not understand tins mysterious book, much, less could the above mentioned writers.

11. ON THE MYSTICAL STONES OF THE CITY OF GOD.

1. If thou be wise.
2. St. Teresa mentions in her " Life," having seen in Purgatory the souls of many persons of remarkable virtue; some in a secular, others in a religious state, of her own, nunnery and of several other orders; though she says, their penitential and holy lives, their patience, their great regularity in their convent, their tears and humility at their death, had persuaded her they would be admitted straight to glory. " But," (she continues,) "amongst all the souls I have seen, I have not known any one to have escaped purgatory except three, F. Peter of Alcantara, F. Peter Ivagnez, a religious man of the order of St. Dominic, and a Carmelite Friar." (See her own life, chap. 38, translated by the pious Mr. Woodhead. 2 vols. 4to. 1669)

6. ON THE FIRST GATE OF THE HOUSE OF GOD, WHICH IS FAITH.

1. Besides many more.

9. ON HUMILITY, WHICH IS THE FOURTH GATE.

1. And thus lose eternal life, and their temporal one at the same time.

10. MORE CONSIDERATIONS ON FAITH.

1. Since in this book it has been our endeavour to inflame the minds of the faithful with a desire of our most delightful and happy country.

5. ON THE JOY OF THE EYES.

1. To whose splendour we shall be made conformable.

6. ON THE JOY OF THE EARS.

1. In his " Life" of St. Francis, chap. v.

1. ON THE TREASURE HIDDEN IN A FIELD.

1. Which is found in St. Matthew.

2. ON THE PRECIOUS PEARL.

1. As he himself tells us.

3. THE LABOURERS IN THE VINEYARD.

1. Though this seems to signify admiration rather than complaint.

4. ON THE TALENTS.

1. Homily 48th. on St. Matthew

St. Robert Francis Romulus Bellarmine

(Also, "Bellarmino").

A distinguished Jesuit theologian, writer, and cardinal, born at Montepulciano, 4 October, 1542; died 17 September, 1621. His father was Vincenzo Bellarmino, his mother Cinthia Cervini, sister of Cardinal Marcello Cervini, afterwards Pope Marcellus II. He was brought up at the newly founded Jesuit college in his native town, and entered the Society of Jesus on 20 September, 1560, being admitted to his first vows on the following day. The next three years he spent in studying philosophy at the Roman College, after which he taught the humanities first at Florence, then at Mondovi. In 1567 he began his theology at Padua, but in 1569 was sent to finish it at Louvain, where he could obtain a fuller acquaintance with the prevailing heresies. Having been ordained there, he quickly obtained a reputation both as a professor and a preacher, in the latter capacity drawing to his pulpit both Catholics and Protestants, even from distant parts. In 1576 he was recalled to Italy, and entrusted with the chair of Controversies recently founded at the Roman College. He proved himself equal to the arduous task, and the lectures thus delivered grew into the work "De Controversiis" which, amidst so much else of excellence, forms the chief title to his greatness. This monumental work was the earliest attempt to systematize the various controversies of the time, and made an immense impression throughout Europe, the blow it dealt to Protestantism being so acutely felt in Germany and England that special chairs were founded in order to provide replies to it. Nor has it even yet been superseded as the classical book on its subject-matter, though, as was to be expected, the progress of criticism has impaired the value of some of its historical arguments.

In 1588 Bellarmine was made Spiritual Father to the Roman College, but in 1590 he went with Cardinal Gaetano as theologian to the embassy Sixtus V was then sending into France to protect the interests of the Church amidst the troubles of the civil wars. Whilst he was there news reached him that Sixtus, who had warmly accepted the dedication of his "De Controversiis", was now proposing to put its first volume on the Index. This was because he had discovered that it assigned to the Holy See not a direct but only an indirect power over temporals. Bellarmine, whose loyalty to the Holy See was intense, took this greatly to heart; it was, however, averted by the death of Sixtus, and the new pope, Gregory XIV, even granted to Bellarmine's work the distinction of a special approbation. Gaetano's mission now terminating, Bellarmine resumed his work as Spiritual Father, and had the consolation of guiding the last years of St. Aloysius Gonzaga, who died in the Roman College in 1591. Many years later he had the further consolation of successfully promoting the beatification of the saintly youth. Likewise at this time he sat on the final commission for the revision of the Vulgate text. This revision had been desired by the Council of Trent, and subsequent popes had laboured over the task and had almost brought it to completion. But Sixtus V, though unskilled in this branch of criticism, had introduced alterations of his own, all for the worse. He had even gone so far as to have an impression of this vitiated edition printed and partially distributed, together with the proposed Bull enforcing its use. He died, however, before the actual promulgation, and his immediate successors at once proceeded to remove the blunders and call in the defective impression. The difficulty was how to substitute a more correct edition without affixing a stigma to the name of Sixtus, and Bellarmine proposed that the new edition should continue in the name of Sixtus, with a prefatory explanation that, on account of *aliqua vitia vel typographorum vel aliorum* which had crept in, Sixtus had himself resolved that a new impression should be undertaken. The suggestion was accepted, and Bellarmine himself wrote the preface, still prefixed to the Clementine edition ever since in use. On the other hand, he has been accused of untruthfulness in stating that Sixtus had resolved on a new impression. But his testimony, as there is no evidence to the contrary, should be accepted as decisive, seeing how conscientious a man he was in the estimation of his contemporaries; and the more so since it cannot be impugned without casting a slur on the character of his fellow-commissioners who accepted his suggestion, and of Clement VIII who with full knowledge of the facts gave his sanction to Bellarmine's preface being prefixed to the new edition. Besides, Angelo Rocca, the Secretary of the revisory commissions of Sixtus V and the succeeding pontiffs, himself wrote a draft preface for the new edition in which he makes the same statement: (Sixtus) "*dum errores ex typographib ortos, et mutationes omnes, atque varias hominum opiniones recognoscere c**oe*pit, ut postea de toto negotio deliberare atque Vulgatam editionem, prout debebat, publicare posset, morte prfventus quod cœperat perficere non potuit*". This draft preface, to which Bellarmine's was preferred, is still extant, attached to the copy of the Sixtine edition in which the Clementine corrections are marked, and may be seen in the Biblioteca Angelica at Rome.

In 1592 Bellarmine was made Rector of the Roman College, and in 1595 Provincial of Naples. In 1597 Clement VIII recalled him to Rome and made him his own theologian and likewise Examiner of Bishops and Consultor of the Holy Office. Further, in 1599 he made him Cardinal-Priest of the title of Santa Maria *in viâ*, alleging as his reason for this promotion that "the Church of God had not his equal in learning". He was now appointed, along with the Dominican Cardinal d'Ascoli, an assessor to Cardinal Madruzzi, the President of the Congregation *de Auxiliis*, which had been instituted shortly before to settle the controversy which had recently arisen between the Thomists and the Molinists concerning the nature of the concord between efficacious grace and human liberty. Bellarmine's advice was from the first that the doctrinal question should not be decided authoritatively, but left over for further discussion in the schools, the disputants on either side being strictly forbidden to indulge in censures or condemnations of their adversaries. Clement VIII at first inclined to this view, but afterwards changed completely and determined on a doctrinal definition. Bellarmine's presence then became embarrassing, and he appointed him to the Archbishopric of Capua just then vacant. This is sometimes spoken of as the cardinal's disgrace, but Clement consecrated him with his own hands—an honour which the popes usually accord as a mark of special regard. The new archbishop departed at once for his see, and during the next three years set a bright example of pastoral zeal in its administration.

In 1605 Clement VIII died, and was succeeded by Leo XI who reigned only twenty-six days, and then by Paul V. In both conclaves, especially that latter, the name of Bellarmine was much before the electors, greatly to his own distress, but his quality as a Jesuit stood against him in the judgment of many of the cardinals. The new pope insisted on keeping him at Rome, and the cardinal, obediently complying, demanded that at least he should be released from an episcopal charge the duties of which he could no longer fulfil. He was now made a member of the Holy Office and of other congregations, and thenceforth was the chief advisor of the Holy See in the theological department of its administration. Of the particular transactions with which his name is most generally associated the following were the most important: The inquiry *de Auxiliis*, which after all Clement had not seen his way to decide, was now terminated with a settlement on the lines of Bellarmine's original suggestion. 1606 marked the beginning of the quarrel between the Holy See and the Republic of Venice which, without even consulting the pope, had presumed to abrogate the law of clerical exemption from civil jurisdiction and to withdraw the Church's right to hold real property. The quarrel led to a war of pamphlets in which the part of the Republic was sustained by John Marsiglio and an apostate monk named Paolo Sarpi, and that of the Holy See by Bellarmine and Baronius. Contemporaneous with the Venetian episode was that of the English Oath of Alliance. In 1606, in addition to the grave disabilities which already weighed them down, the English Catholics were required under pain of *præmunire* to take an oath of allegiance craftily worded in such wise that a Catholic in refusing to take it might appear to be disavowing an undoubted civl obligation, whilst if he should take it he would be not merely rejecting but even condemning as "impious and heretical" the doctrine of the deposing power, that is to say, of a power, which, whether rightly or wrongly, the Holy See had claimed and exercised for centuries with the full approval of Christendom, and which even in that age the mass of the theologians of Europe defended. The Holy See having forbidden Catholics to take this oath, King James himself came forward as its defender, in a book entitled "Tripoli nodo triplex cuneus", to which Bellarmine replied in his "Responsio Matthfi Torti". Other treatises followed on either side, and the result of one, written in denial of the deposing power by William Barclay, an English jurist resident in France, was that Bellarmine's reply to it was branded by the Regalist *Parlement* of Paris. Thus it came to pass that, for following the *via media* of the indirect power, he was condemned in 1590 as too much of a Regalist and in 1605 as too much of a Papalist.

Bellarmine did not live to deal with the later and more serious stage of the Galileo case, but in 1615 he took part in its earlier stage. He had always shown great interest in the discoveries of that investigator, and was on terms of friendly correspondence with him. He took up too—as is witnessed by his letter to Galileo's friend Foscarini—exactly the right attitude towards scientific theories in seeming contradiction with Scripture. If, as was undoubtedly the case then with Galileo's heliocentric theory, a scientific theory is insufficiently proved, it should be advanced only as an hypothesis; but if, as is the case with this theory now, it is solidly demonstrated, care must be taken to interpret Scripture only in accordance with it. When the Holy Office condemned the heliocentric theory, by an excess in the opposite direction, it became Bellarmine's official duty to signify the condemnation to Galileo, and receive his submission. Bellarmine lived to see one more conclave, that which elected Gregory XV (February, 1621). His health was now failing, and in the summer of the same year he was permitted to retire to Sant' Andrea and prepare for the end. His death was most edifying and was a fitting termination to a life which had been no less remarkable for its virtues than for its achievements.

His spirit of prayer, his singular delicacy of conscience and freedom from sin, his spirit of humility and poverty, together with the disinterestedness which he displayed as much under the cardinal's robes as under the Jesuit's gown, his lavish charity to the poor, and his devotedness to work, had combined to impress those who knew him intimately with the feeling that he was of the number of the saints. Accordingly, when he died there was a general expectation that his cause would be promptly introduced. And so it was, under Urban VIII in 1627, when he became entitled to the appellation of Venerable. But a technical obstacle, arising out of Urban VIII's own general legislation in regard to beatifications, required its prorogation at that time. Though it was reintroduced on several occasions (1675, 1714, 1752, and 1832), and though on each occasion the great preponderance of votes was in favour of the beatification, a successful issue came only after many years. This was partly because of the influential character of some of those who recorded adverse votes, Barbarigo, Casante, and Azzolino in 1675, and Passionei in 1752, but still more for reasons of political expediency, Bellarmine's name being closely associated with a doctrine of papal authority most obnoxious to the Regalist politicians of the French Court. "We have said", wrote Benedict XIV to Cardinal de Tencin, "in confidence to the General of the Jesuits that the delay of the Cause has come not from the petty matters laid to his charge by Cardinal Passionei, but from the sad circumstances of the times" (Études Religieuses, 15 April, 1896).

Writings of Bellarmine

A full list of Bellarmine's writings, and of those directed against him, may be seen in Sommervogel's "Bibliothèque de la compagnie de Jésus". The following are the principal:

• *Controversial works*. "Disputationes de Controversiis Christianae Fidei adversus hujus temporis hereticos", of the innumerable editions of which the chief are those of Ingolstadt (1586-89), Venice (1596), revised personally by the author, but abounding in printer's errors, Paris or "Triadelphi" (1608), Prague (1721), Rome (1832); "De Exemptione clericorum", and "De Indulgentiis et Jubilaeo", published as monographs in 1599, but afterwards incorporated in the "De Controversiis"; "De Transitu Romani Imperii a Graecis ad Francos" (1584); "Responsio ad praecipua capita Apologiae . . . pro successione Henrici Navarreni" (1586); "Judicium de Libro quem Lutherani vocant Concordiae" (1585); four *Risposte* to the writings on behalf of the Venetian Republic of John Marsiglio and Paolo Sarpi (1606); "Responsio Matthaei Torti ad librum inscriptum Triplici nodo triplex cuneus" 1608); "Apologia Bellarmini pro responsi one sub ad librum Ja-

255

cobi Magnae Britanniae Regis" (1609); Tractatus de potestate Summi Pontificis in rebus temporalibus, adversus Gulielmum Barclay" (1610).

• *Catechetical and Spiritual Works*. "Dottrina Cristiana breve", and "Dichiarazione più copiosa della dottrina cristiana" (1598), two catechetical works which have more than once received papal approbation, and have been translated into various languages; "Dichiarazione del Simbolo" (1604), for the use of priests; "Admonitio ad Episcopum Theanensem nepotem suum quae sint necessaria episcopo" (1612); "Exhortationes domesticae", published only in 1899, by Pére van Ortroy; "*Conciones habitae Lovanii*", the more correct edition (1615); "De Ascensione mentis in Deum" (1615); "De Aeterna felicitate sanctorum" (1616); "De gemitu columbae" (1617); "De septem verbis Christi" (1618); "De arte bene moriendi" (1620). The last five are spiritual works written during his annual retreats.

• *Exegetical and other works*. "De Scriptoribus ecclesiasticis" (1615); "De Editione Latinae Vulgatae, quo sensu a Concilio Tridentino definitum sit ut ea pro authenticae habeatur", not published till 1749; "In omnes Psalmos dilucida expositio" (1611). Complete editions of Bellarmine's *Opera omnia* have been published at Cologne (1617); Venice (1721); Naples (1856); Paris (1870).

Ven. R. Bellarmini, S.R.E. Cardinalis, vita quam ipse scripsit (with an Appendix), written in 1613, at the request of Fathers Eudfmon Joannis and Mutius Vitelleschi, first published among the *acta* of the Process of Beatification 1675; republished in 1887 by DÖLLINGER AND REUSCH, with notes many of which are useful but the general tone of which is unfair and spiteful; a multitude of unpublished documents in the archives of the Vatican, Simancas, Salamanca, the Society of Jesus, etc.; *Epistolæ familiares* (1650); EUDAEMON JOANNIS, *De pio obitu Card. Bellarmini* (1621); FINALI, *Esame fatto per me*, that is, by the lay brother who attended him in his last sickness, MS.; lives by FULIGATI (1624; translated into Latin with additions by PETRA SANCTA, 1626) and BARTOLI, (1678); CERVINI, *Imago virtutum* (1625). These form the chief original material. Of derived lives the best are those by FRIZON (1708), and COUDERC (1893). See also LE BACHELET IN VACANT, *Dict. de thiol. cath.*; and for Bellarmine's doctrine on papal authority, DE LA SERVIÈRE, *De Jacobo Angl. Rege cum Card. R. Bellarmine . . . disputante* (1900).

SYDNEY F. SMITH
Catholic Encyclopedia, 1913

Also Available

www.ingramcontent.com/pod-product-compliance
Lightning Source LLC
Chambersburg PA
CBHW020319160726
47992CB00004B/1610